Carmel, New York.
September 25, 1920.

From Miss Genevieve Mooney.

25 Shepherd Av.
Brooklyn.

J-Th. Vénard
m.s.

A MODERN MARTYR

THEOPHANE VÉNARD
(BLESSED)

REVISED AND ANNOTATED BY THE

VERY REV. JAMES A. WALSH, M. AP.

CATHOLIC FOREIGN MISSION SOCIETY,
MARYKNOLL, OSSINING P. O., NEW YORK

Imprimatur:

✠ John Cardinal Farley

Archbishop of New York

"The world martyrs the Church, and the Church subdues the world. The words of our Divine Lord are always verified, 'I come not to send peace upon earth, but a sword.' The age of martyrs, as of miracles, never ceases. Martyrdom is a perpetual note upon the Mystical Body, which has the Stigmata of Jesus ever fresh upon it."—*Cardinal Wiseman.*

SIXTH EDITION

𝕯𝖊𝖉𝖎𝖈𝖆𝖙𝖎𝖔𝖓

———

This edition of Blessed Theophane Vénard's life is dedicated to the Catholic youth of America in the hope and belief that among them many will be found to follow Christ the whole way into the wilderness for the souls that He has died to save.

CONTENTS.

Preface.

LIST OF ILLUSTRATIONS.

PREFACE.

In the city of Paris on the 5th day of June, 1852, two young men were ordained to the priesthood. One, born in Ireland twenty-three years before, was appointed almost immediately to the chair of Fundamental Dogma in the Seminary of St. Sulpice at Paris. Nineteen years later, during the revolt of the Communists, this priest, from his prison cell in the Conciergerie, defied his persecutors and narrowly escaped massacre. Afterwards, in 1884, he came to America and, until his death in 1900, gave to the clergy of the United States the ripened fruit of his broad and cultured mind.

The other young man, a native of France, was ordained for the foreign missions of Eastern Asia, and four months later sailed for Tong-king, at the southeast extremity of China, where, after seven years of apostolic labor, he was beheaded for the faith.

These two young men were John Baptist Hogan, the late honored superior of St. John's Seminary in Boston, and Jean Theophane Vénard, now Blessed, the subject of these letters.

To Father Hogan, his early guide in the spiritual life, the editor of this volume is indebted for a first acquaintance with the story of Theophane Vénard, whose letters, read in Seminary days at Brighton, have always been a treasured memory.

In the summer of 1903, while at the Paris Seminary for Foreign Missions, he learned that Theophane's youngest brother, Eusebius, was still living, and at once arranged to visit him.

He found Eusebius a venerable priest, curé of the

little village of Assai, in the diocese of Poitiers. With this visit began a cordial friendship, which became more intimate through subsequent correspondence and two later sojourns in the province of Deux-Sèvres.

In Assai and at St. Loup, the martyr's birthplace, a few miles away, were secured most of the photographs and extra data that appear in this volume.

A few weeks after his first visit to Assai the writer called, in London, upon the late Lady Herbert of Lea, to whom English-speaking Catholics are indebted for the discovery of the charming letters which make up this life. When Lady Herbert learned of the writer's intention to publish these letters anew, she expressed the hope that her former work, which had long been out of print, might be of some service.

Lady Herbert's kindness was accepted and many of the letters which appeared in the earlier translation were embodied substantially in this new life.

CATHOLIC FOREIGN MISSION SEMINARY, MARYKNOLL, N. Y.
Feast of the Presentation, November 21, 1913.

FROM LADY HERBERT'S PREFACE.

"Theophane Vénard was no ascetic saint, trembling at every manifestation of human or natural feeling. He was eminently a tender and dutiful son; a most devoted and loving brother; an equally devoted and attached friend. Neither did he consider these warm affections incompatible with the great work to which he had given his life. His devotion to his sister, whom he calls 'part of his very life,' shines through every page of this touching and beautiful correspondence. She is the first thought of his boyish years, she is his last thought in death. Yet all this strong human love did not prevent his sacrificing everything to God —leaving the home he loved so fondly, the sister he idolized, the family tie which bound him with what others might have considered iron links,—everything, in fact, which made life dear,—when the voice of the Master called him to go forth from his people and his country into a strange and distant land, to preach His word and do His work, and save the souls for whom He died upon the Cross. This is the striking characteristic of the life before us—human love, surpassing all ordinary home affections, willingly and joyfully offered up on the altar of our Lord for the salvation of the heathen who knew Him not."

LADY HERBERT'S TRIBUTE.

"Herbert House,
Belgrave Square, S. W.,
January 4, 1906.

"Dear Father Walsh:—

"I am delighted with the beautiful new edition of Theophane Vénard's Life, which you so kindly sent to me, and which reached me on New Year's Day. It is so infinitely superior to the original that they cannot be compared, and the insertion of the pictures gives an additional interest to it.

"Cardinal Vaughan, years ago, asked me to put a penny edition of the 'Life' among the publications of the Catholic Truth Society, so that Theophane Vénard's glorious example might be followed by many English lads; and it answered admirably. It has been sold more largely than almost any other of the penny pamphlets.

"I am very grateful to you for having brought out this excellent biography of one so dear to all who love the foreign missions, which are more dear to me than any other Catholic work.

"Yours with many grateful thanks, and much respect,

Very sincerely,
M. E. HERBERT."

A MODERN MARTYR

(*THEOPHANE VÉNARD*)

CHAPTER I.

Birth and School Days.

St. Loup-sur-Thouet is a little French town in the department of Deux-Sèvres, in the diocese of Poitiers, situated some miles north of Parthenay. Here begins the beautiful golden valley which gives its name to Airvault (aurea vallis), a busy little town built in the shape of an amphitheatre, and possessing, besides the ruins of an old castle, a very interesting Gothic church. Airvault is not more than three miles from St. Loup, which, surrounded by numerous hills, is hardly discernible even at a short distance.

In spite of the ill-natured assertions of a modern author, the population of St. Loup is too serious and religious to have imbibed any Voltairian spirit. Even should it be true that the author of "Henriade" was born there, St. Loup now boasts of a more glorious hero; for from its soil has sprung in these latter days, —a martyr.

Jean Theophane Vénard was born at St. Loup on the 21st of November, 1829, the feast of the Presentation of the Blessed Virgin. He belonged to one of those patriarchal families in which religion and honor hold the first place. His father, M. Jean Vénard,

1

whose family came originally from Anjou, filled the post of village school-master with as much ability as devotion to his duties. He gave up this fatiguing work only after thirty years of toil, to accept a position as justice of the peace in the department of which St. Loup was the chief town. There his experience in business and his good judgment made him invaluable to his townspeople, until the day when his laborious and useful labors were brought to a close.

His wife, Mme. Marie Guéret, was a gentle, pious woman, simple and loving in character, entirely devoted to the care of her own home. She had six children. Two of these died as infants, but the others, Mélanie, Theophane, Henry, and Eusebius, will all play an important part in this little history. Under the direction of these good parents, Theophane Vénard made rapid progress in virtue. He combined the loving, gentle character of his mother with the firmness and resolution of his father. His contemporaries still talk of the amusing contrast between his small, baby figure and his grave, quiet manner. His greatest pleasure was to watch the goats or the cows on the hillside, an occupation which fostered his love of solitude and his spirit of recollection. These hillsides and pleasant fields hold an important place in the story of the future missioner, for here the first thoughts of his vocation came upon him; and the feelings then inspired remained among the sweetest of his whole life.

The country around St. Loup is very picturesque, but it owes its great fertility to the rivers, the Thouet and the Cebron, which intersect the valley in opposite directions. Between the beds of these two rivers is a hillside called "Le Bel-Air," on account of its healthful situation and the glorious view on all sides. When Theophane was only nine years old, his delight was to

pasture his father's goats on this spot with his sister
or a friend. Here they would sing, or read books
which they had borrowed from the pastor of the
village. Among these books, the "Annals of the
Propagation of the Faith" had the greatest charm for
the little boy. One day he was reading aloud to his
companions the life of the Venerable Charles Cornay,
whose martyrdom was then recent. The account of
·the sufferings and death of this martyr for Jesus
Christ touched him even to tears, so that at the end he
cried out, "And I too will go to Tong-king, and I too
will be a martyr!"

Shortly afterwards his father joined the little group,
and Theophane, turning to him with a gravity very
unusual at his age, said, "My father, how much is this
field worth?" "Well, I really don't know exactly, my
child," replied his father. "Why do you ask?" "Because," the boy answered, "if you could give it to
me, and I could have it for my share, I would sell it,
and then I should be able to go to college and study."
His father, surprised at such serious thoughts in one
so young, put him off with some simple answer; but
he thought over these words which gave him a new
light on the character and intentions of his son. He
soon allowed the boy to learn Latin with one or two
other children who went for that purpose to the presbytery, and Theophane succeeded so well that it was
decided to send him to college for a regular course
of study.

At this time, the principal of the College of Doué, in
the diocese of Angers, was a brother of the venerable
pastor of St. Loup, and to him young Vénard was sent
in October, 1841, together with a friend whom he had
known and loved from childhood. This friendship
never cooled, and ten years afterwards Theophane

wrote from Paris,—"Until I came to the Séminaire des Missions Étrangères, the only intimate friend I ever had was one who had been born in my own village, and who was dear to me as my own soul. The same fatherly hand baptized us; side by side we sat on our benches at school; and at the very same time we were transplanted together to a new home, where another father received us both with open arms. My friend was older, cleverer, and wiser than I, and took a higher place in the College, but our friendship was not in the least affected by this. He flew, and I crawled; but we were each quite contented. I was transferred to the 'Petit Séminaire'*; and there we found each other again in the same cloister, sharing the same masters, the same studies, the same companions. God, who had united us in childhood, gave us but one thought, one aim, and one object in life. But the day at last came when we were to be separated— my life seemed to be broken altogether! But I have the firm hope that we shall be reunited in Heaven."

No sooner was he fairly settled at college, than Theophane gave his whole mind to the fulfilment of his duties. He was a model to the other students, not only through the hours of study but also during recreation, when he showed himself the gayest of the whole party. He bore all ill-nature or contradiction with such good humor that those who were at first inclined to tease him soon gave it up. The more people vexed him, or gave him pain, the greater was his kindness toward them, and he rarely failed to win their hearts and make them ashamed of their previous behavior.

He gladly entered into all the little private devo-

---

*Preparatory Seminary.

tions of the students, which were in harmony with his taste and affections. Even as a child he had vowed a special devotion to the Blessed Virgin. He was inscribed among the children of Mary, at Notre Dame des Victoires, and enrolled himself in the work of the Propagation of the Faith, determined to help missioners as far as he could, until he became one himself. He tried also to lead, as much as he was permitted, a mortified life. When, on a winter's day, one of the masters, seeing him suffer very much from chilblains on his hands and feet, told him to go and warm himself by the comfortable fire in his room, Theophane refused, exclaiming, "The missioners you were talking to us about last night, sir, suffered much more than that!"

He had a passion for reading, and delighted in the lives of children of his own age, and especially of those who had suffered martyrdom. All these holy dispositions were fostered by the thoughts of his first Communion, which was approaching, and for which, unlike the average small boy, he prepared himself with the utmost anxiety and care.

"The day has almost come," he wrote his parents, "that day which I have so earnestly desired! the most beautiful day in my whole life! Please pray to the Blessed Virgin for me, that I may receive her Son worthily, for I feel I can never prepare myself sufficiently for so solemn an occasion. I beg you, therefore, to forgive me any faults I may have committed against you, and to give me your blessing."

Great as had been his previous doubts and fears, when the time came, his joy knew no bounds. "I remember him perfectly on that day," wrote one of his tutors. "He seemed not able to contain himself for happiness." From that hour began his great devo-

tion to the Blessed Sacrament. He would steal away
for a visit during recreation. "I often used to open
the door of the chapel softly to see if he was there,"
wrote the same master, "and was always edified by
his wonderful spirit of recollection. Sometimes I
forced him to go out to play with his companions, as
I thought it necessary for his health; then devotion
gave place to obedience."

But a great sorrow was hanging over his head, for
which he would need all the strength his Lord had
vouchsafed to him in the Sacrament of His love.
After two happy months spent with his family, he was
obliged to part with his mother to return to college,
and he foresaw that their parting would be a final
one. Very soon after, in fact, she expired calmly in
the arms of her husband, leaving him the care of their
four little children. The blow to Theophane was
terrible. Nevertheless, his first thought was how he
could best console the mourners at home.

"Dearest papa," he writes, "when you wrote me
that my darling mother was very weak and suffering,
I flattered myself that our prayers and tears would
win from God the preservation of her life. But just
now the headmaster has told me of the terrible misfortune which has befallen us. O my God, help me to
say, 'Thy Will be done!' The hour fixed by Him has
come and she has had to leave us, and is gone to be
our protector in Heaven with the two little angels to
whom she gave birth. Once more, may His Holy
Name be blessed! It is thus He tries His creatures
here below. Putting on the buckler of faith, we will
have recourse to religion, which alone can comfort
us in such sorrows. But it is very, very bitter. I have
cried till I can cry no longer, and I have prayed with
all my heart for her dear soul. May she at this mo-

ment be in the enjoyment of the Beatific Vision with His elect! May the Saviour whom she ever loved and whom she strove to serve, receive her into His kingdom!"

But our Lord reserved to Theophane a special consolation. Many years after the event, and at the moment when he was about to leave his family forever, he broke silence on the subject, and said, "I think I may assure you positively that our good mother is in Heaven. I tell you this for your comfort; but I have never spoken of it before, and I must beg of you not to repeat it to any one. At the time of her death, one night when I was watching in prayer, an angel took me by the hand and led me, as it were, into a great and wonderful Light, in the midst of which, surrounded by other glorified bodies, I distinctly saw her whom we so fondly loved, and for whom we had wept so bitterly."

From the time of this great sorrow the links which bound brother and sister were drawn closer, and a correspondence began between Theophane and his sister, Mélanie, which ceased only with death. Their letters remain as models of tenderness and holy inspirations, while they are most attractive in point of style and taste. Speaking on this subject, the Bishop of Poitiers says, "It is in this outpouring of heart to heart that we see his extreme delicacy of feeling, his loving thoughtfulness, his graceful imagination, and the good judgment which balanced all his other qualities. We have read these letters again and again, with ever-increasing pleasure, and we trust we shall be forgiven if we have watered some of them with our tears."

In the course of the winter of 1844, Theophane writes, "I must send you a few lines, my dearest sister, for there is not a day, nor scarcely an hour, when I

do not think of you, who are so very dear to me. I
know you too are thinking of me, and I suppose you
will be saying, 'Oh, my poor old brother will be so
cold this winter; and here am I enjoying a good big
fire!' Be comforted. Though I have suffered from
the cold, as you know I always do, yet I have had some
fun out of it too, for we have had famous skating.
And now the weather is milder, and I am thawing,
and pouring out some of my thoughts to my second
self."

Soon after, his brother Henry joined Theophane at
the College; and it was impossible not to be touched
at the care which the elder took of the younger, so as
to spare him the usual schoolboy troubles. In 1845,
the Sodality of the Children of Mary was established
in the College, and Theophane announced this event
with joy to his sister. He was made sacristan of his
chapel, an honor which he greatly coveted, as it not
only gave him the care of the altar, but enabled him
to steal away oftener for prayer. "Yesterday," he
wrote to Mélanie, "I went to say my rosary in the
chapel; and I don't know why, but I was very sad,
and I began to cry like a child. Yet all the time I had
a wonderful interior consolation, and everything
appeared to me in a supernatural light. . . . Very
often, when I am at work, my thoughts fly back to
you. I seem to see you going lightly about the house,
singing softly as is your wont, and doing things for
our father and the children and everybody. I follow
you in thought everywhere. Although we are so far
apart, our thoughts, our wishes, our aspirations seem to
be one. Oh, what a blessed thing it is, this communion
of souls, to be able to pray for each other, and to pray
for our loved ones together! A sort of peace and
calm comes over me with this thought. Do you know,

the other day, on the Feast of our Patron Saint, as I was kneeling before the Blessed Sacrament at Benediction, the Blessed Virgin seemed to smile amidst her flowers and tapers, and I thought of you, who, I know, were then at the Sodality Vespers. I prayed so hard for you, and I felt that you were doing the same for me and that our prayers were one. And then I was so happy, so relieved. But I should like to be with you again in body as well as in spirit. Oh, when shall we cease to be separated? When shall we be able to live together as we did as children and share all our troubles and all our joys?"

It seemed as if a vision of the future were before him—that future which was to be so great a struggle to flesh and blood. But we must not anticipate.

CHAPTER II.

At College—Doué and Montmorillon.

On New Year's Eve, 1847, Theophane wrote to his father from Doué:—

"Here we are in the midst of piercing frost and cold; but if the winter numbs our limbs, at least it does not freeze our hearts. Whatever happens—whether my chilblains disappear or not—I can't let New Year's Day pass without scribbling a few lines to repeat once more to you my hearty prayers and wishes for your happiness. People declare that New Year's Day is the day for telling lies. Let those say so who tell them. As for me I always welcome the return of the anniversary as an occasion for renewing the expressions of my old childhood's love. In one word, dearest papa, I wish you many, many happy New Years."

At this time Theophane was eighteen. Although he had given himself up to God from his youth, the devil filled him with doubts and temptations when it came to a question of deciding on his future vocation, and, as usual, his sister is the confidante of his troubles:—

"My dearest Mélanie,—We must talk a little of the Blessed Virgin, for I feel as if I had not spoken enough of her this year. Can it be that I have changed? I think not; but other thoughts preoccupy me just now. I am nearly at the end of my classes here and yet I seem to have no clear conception of my future. This worries me very much. I always thought I was called to the priesthood. Sometimes I say to myself, 'What a glorious thing it is to be a priest! What it must mean to say one's first Mass!' But then for that, one must be so good!—so pure!—like one of God's angels. That is why I still hesitate. Please to unite your prayers with mine, that I may discern God's will in the matter. Will you? But why do I ask? I know you will, and I want you to give me your Communion the first Sunday in Lent with this intention, and I will prepare myself for the same."

A little later he writes, "O my dearest sister, do write to me at once, for I look only to you for comfort. Bring back hope to my poor sad heart; that is your mission, you know. As regards me, I should like to laugh and be merry with you; but I have not the heart. I wait for your letter with the greatest anxiety."

Still his heart turned towards Mary in the midst of his greatest distresses: "O Mary, how I love the word! Mary, refuge of sorrowful hearts! Mary, under whose wing we have both sheltered ourselves, like little children with their mother at the approach of the enemy! I love Mary, but I think you, my dearest sister, love her more." . . . Then he comes back to his previous sorrow. "I get so weary of life and of everything, I don't know what to do. It is only to you that I dare own such a thing. But you, you are half of myself. You are more than my sister—you are my guardian angel."

At last, by God's grace, peace came back to his soul, and he writes,—

"Dearest Mélanie,—Thank you, my good little sister, thank you a thousand times for your delicious letter. Oh what good it has done me! Once more I thank you with all my heart, that's all I can say. Here is the month of Mary nearly over! It is high time we should talk about her a little. We too have special devotions every day for Mary's month, and I delight in decorating her altar. We have a quantity of beautiful roses in the garden here. The largest and sweetest, you may be sure, I keep for our tender, good Mother, and it is a great pleasure to offer her fresh ones every morning. I fear the hands and the heart that bring them are miserably unworthy; but she is so good, she receives everybody! Well may we call her 'Comfort of the Afflicted' and 'Refuge of Sinners.'

"Oh, if you did but know how my poor old head works when I am all alone, and can't sleep for thinking! Oh, how happy I should be in a quiet country parish with my Mélanie! I would guide the good people to try to save their souls, and you would have care of the church; and together we would labor for God, and talk of Him and of His Mother, and of all those we have loved and lost. But one thought troubles me in the midst of these castles in the air. All this is very good and very pleasant certainly; but when it comes to the point, what is the Priesthood? Is it not an entire detachment from all worldly goods—a complete abandonment of all temporal interests? To be a Priest, one should be a Saint. To guide others, one must first learn to guide oneself. Then should not the life of a good Priest be one of continual sacrifice, self-immolation, and mortification of all kinds? How in the world should I ever have the courage to embrace such a life,—I who am so little advanced in the paths of virtue, or of penance?

"These are my thoughts, darling sister, and they always come back to the same thing.

"But when I pray God to enlighten me, I seem to hear an interior voice ever singing, 'Thou must be a Priest; God gives His grace to all who ask Him.' Then a great peace seems to come over me, and I find myself happy and contented. You will say, 'What on earth am I to conclude from all this?' Why, that the choice of a vocation is a terrible thing, and that whoever thinks of it seriously is in a desperate difficulty.

"But as concerns myself, I hope, in spite of my unworthiness, that God will have pity upon me. Our God is a Father, and a most tender Father; and we have besides a powerful Advocate in one who deigns to be our Mother."

But in Mélanie's own heart the struggle was going on likewise as to the choice of a vocation, and the mutual difficulties and the entire confidence which they had in each other bound them, if possible, still more closely. In Theophane's mind his sister appeared more and more holy, while his own love for God was unconsciously increasing in like proportion.

He writes again to her, "You may be quite sure that I am true to my promise, and if you pray for me I feel often as if my life were one prayer for you. But though you will laugh at me for saying so, I can't help sometimes, when I am asking God and His saints to enlighten us, I can't help, I say, wishing for what you do not desire. I hear you say, 'But this is not right; this is not really loving me.' Don't be angry, the thought is repented of as soon as conceived. But the fact is, I cannot bear the idea of a total separation. I am afraid this arises from selfishness on my part; never mind, it is only a slight shade. No, dearest Mé-

lanie! believe this,—I will never try for an instant to
turn you from any generous or holy project. I should
be afraid of robbing you of your crown! But I tell
you frankly that to lose you would be a terrible sacrifice on my part. Every time the thought comes across
my mind, I beg for the grace of God to enable me to
bear it, if it be His will that you should go and leave
us. I wish only for your highest happiness. You say
that God calls you. If so, so much the better for you!
I can only envy you your lot, and hope that some day
I may have the like favor. Let us leave it to our dear
Lord and Master to direct our future; our only business is to strive to correspond with His grace as far
as we possibly can."

Theophane was going upwards with rapid strides,
and not content with the Priesthood, was beginning to
thirst after the higher glories of the Apostolate. He
himself said later that he was, as it were, led by the
hand, not knowing whither he was going. The following memorandum, found among his copy-books,
and dated June 17th, 1847, shows the working of his
mind at that time:—

"To-day in the chapel of the College at Doué, I
made a vow to Mary, Refuge of Sinners, to say my
rosary every day, *in order to obtain a special grace
from God.*"

In the following letter to his sister, he gives an enthusiastic description of the procession on the Festival
of Corpus Christi, and concludes with the words, "If
religious services on earth are so glorious, what must
they be in Heaven? Eternity! Have you ever thought
of this word? Eternal, eternal! a thing which
will never, never end! Reflecting on such subjects
sometimes overwhelms me, although I am still

inclined to be giddy and thoughtless. I try occasionally to find some kind of theory about it which I can comprehend; but when I have made my plan I only feel, 'Oh what a goose I am!' and then all my fine building crumbles away."

Theophane had remained six years at the College of Doué, and he already gave promise of great ability. His frank, sweet-tempered nature made him a universal favorite, while his piety, sound judgment, and high principle won the respect and confidence of his tutors. Although kind to every one, he kept his love for his own family and for two or three of his companions; and on these he lavished all the wealth of his affectionate, loving heart. This devotion to his family and to one or two congenial souls far exceeded any ordinary love or friendship, and seemed to be permitted by God in order to show the full power of His grace, which hereafter would wean him from all human ties, and say to him, as to Abraham, "Go forth out of thy country, and from thy kindred, and out of thy father's house, and come into the land which I shall show thee."

As to his person, although under medium height, he had a peculiarly pleasing and taking appearance, with a frank expression, a clear complexion—slightly tinged with red—bright eyes, and a very fascinating manner.* He was above the average in his studies, always bringing home the first prizes, and he had a great talent for poetry and other kinds of composition,

At the vacation in 1847 he left school, and in the

---

*The hair was dark, almost black. The writer has in his possession several relics, brought from St. Loup, and among them are some locks of hair, cut before Theophane's departure. A daguerreotype which formerly hung in the home of Fr. Eusebius Vénard at Assai, gives the truest likeness. [Ed.

month of October entered what is called "Le Petit
Séminaire" at Montmorillon.   He was very happy
here, and wrote to his sister, "From the bottom of my
heart, dearest Mélanie, I do assure you I never was so
happy. . . . †'Cor unum et anima una',—this is the
motto of the congregation!   Such words can come
only from God Himself!   Is not that the link which
unites all Christians to one another?   Is it not this
feeling which creates the Missioner, the Priest, the
Christian Brother, the Sister of Charity?   Cor unum,
we can apply it to ourselves, for our love and our
hopes are one.   Oh, yes!   Cor unum et anima una!
We can say so now, and we shall be able to say so
still better later, if God calls you to serve Him more
distinctly.   Go, go, my dear, good sister.   I will
never stop you, notwithstanding the sorrow I cannot
help feeling at the idea.   But think a little bit of our
father, our dear, good father.   I pray for you every
day, that God may deign to enlighten us both and
to show us His Holy Will."

There was nothing gloomy or repelling in his religion.   On the contrary, he was always cheerful and
merry, especially at Montmorillon, where his *en-
train* and gaiety became proverbial, and where the
little feasts of which he was the presiding genius will
be remembered as long as his generation remains.*

---

†One heart and one mind.

*Montmorillon is only a short journey from Poitiers, and in the
early part of July, 1905, the writer spent a pleasant day and night
at the "petit séminaire."   Several new frescoes adorn the chapel,
one describing in detail the martyrdom of Theophane Vénard, the
others being devoted to two more of the alumni who have also won
the "martyr's crown."   The members of the seminary faculty, a
body of bright, active young diocesan priests, were most gracious
and attentive to the American who was interested in their saintly
pupil, and the students of English on this occasion enjoyed the
novelty of hearing English spoken without a French accent.   The
traditions of the house have hardly changed since Theophane and
Eusebius Vénard lived there.   [Ed.

BOYS AT THE PREPARATORY SEMINARY,
Montmorillon.

In spite of his gaiety and fun, however, Theophane
had a strong groundwork of serious and deep feeling,
which came out in his letters to his little brother, of
which we will give some extracts here:—

"My dear little Eusebius,—Well, how do you like
school? Are the lessons very hard? Very disagreeable? Courage! you are just now at the bottom of the
ladder. Very soon you will get on, and see the fruit
of your work. Have you found any fellows that you
like? Have you jolly games together? Tell me all. I
so often think of my poor little brother and wish I
could be with him, especially in these first weeks of
his school life. . . . It is half-past six in the evening.
The wind blows through the chinks of the door; isn't
it bitter? But I feel so for you, my poor little man. I
am sure your poor little toes and paws are all over
chilblains, as mine used to be; and the tip of your nose
is all frozen, isn't it? Ah! but that's the true life of a
schoolboy! We go to learn to bear; but let us leave
the winter behind, and wish one another a very, very
happy New Year, and Paradise by and by, though I
hope not just yet, as I don't feel disposed to give up
my little brother so soon. I recollect how in old times
you used to long for New Year's Day, but then that
was all for the presents and sugar-plums. Now, alas!
there are no presents and no goodies—only lessons.
Oh, dear! But by and by you will be glad to have
learned something, so as to be more fit to fulfil the duties God will appoint for you in life, and thus win
Heaven. For that, dear Eusebius, and that alone, must
be the object of all our actions. Work hard, work well,
not to get praise, or honor, or prizes, but because you
will thus please God. Take this as the maxim of your
life: 'All for our good God.' Don't neglect your

2

prayers. Be docile to your superiors, for they are set over you by God; be loving and kind to your companions, and then everybody will love you, and you will be really happy."

Then came his little brother's first Communion, and Theophane writes,—

"My dear little brother has just made a great step in life, and a step towards another world. For one little moment you paused and pitched your tent, and looked back to all your childish faults, faults which the world counts little, but which a Christian judges differently; and kneeling at the feet of God's priest, you told him all these little failings and short-comings, and he lifted the burden from your shoulders with the words of absolution in the name of the Thrice Holy God. You have now become once more innocent as a little child, and the friend of the angels; and you have received Him whom the heaven of heavens cannot contain. Oh, the inexpressible happiness of the child's first Communion! Who can describe that mystery of love? Only angels know that language. May you understand it, too, my dear little angel on earth!"*

Theophane was now eighteen. His year of Philosophy was over, and he was about to be transferred from the "Petit" to the "Grand Séminaire," but first he was allowed to go home, and his joy found vent in the following words:—

"In a month more I shall see the sky of my native

---

*Eusebius Vénard was, until his death, February 24, 1913, pastor of Assai, a small town about five miles from the railway station at Airvault, and less than four miles from the paternal home of St. Loup. [Ed.

valley. How happy the thought makes me! My friends at the 'Grand Séminaire' begin their vacation a month sooner, which makes me rather envious. Well, the time will soon slip by. My schoolboy life is at an end; it has not been without its trials, but it has had its sweets too. For the *moment* I feel as if I wanted the fresh air of my own dear home to strengthen me, body and soul. Till now I have not *lived,* so to speak. I am going to begin. Every living thing seems to me to follow its vocation. The river flows to the sea, and the plant germinates, and the animal feeds and grows, and man lives and draws daily nearer to God. But each man walks after his own fashion. The business of one is to cultivate the soil; another, the intellect. Handicrafts supply the material wants of mankind; politics, the social. One and all gravitate towards their end, which is death, although each follows a different path. In one sense man has a free will, but he can scarcely be said to choose his career; it is almost always marked out for him. If he wanders from it, nothing but confusion is the result. Well, I am longing to work and to find my place in the world, to spend and be spent for my brethren. Whatever course be proposed to me, I always come back to that —to be a Priest. No other career has the least attraction for me. Yes, one day I shall be the soldier of Jesus Christ, and fight under the banner of the Church, and the day will soon dawn for the fulfilment of that wish. That is why I feel so happy at the thought of going home soon. A week or two among my own people, and then to my cell and to my vocation forevermore."

CHAPTER III.

The Seminarian at Poitiers.

THEOPHANE VÉNARD entered the "Grand Seminary," as we have seen, with the firm determination to
become a Priest.   He understood at once how important the training there given would be to him; and
the shortness of the time allowed made him grasp at
every opportunity to improve himself, especially as re-
garded his sanctification.   With a clear and subtle intellect, and abilities very much above the common, he
at once distinguished himself among his companions;
but none of these qualities made him lose sight of the
great virtue of humility, which he cultivated assidu-
ously, so as always to try to escape notice by burying
himself among the rest.   He also made charity act as
the handmaid of humility; and therefore not only re-
frained from any unkind act or word, but denied himself many of those little sharp and amusing "repartees"
which his wit and sense of fun made often very tempt-
ing to him.   He preferred to pass for one who was dull
and could not enter into a joke, than to wound in the
smallest degree the feelings of another.   "I think that
this was not the least remarkable of his virtues,"
wrote one of his college friends.

His regularity in his work attracted the attention of
all his masters; and he even began to have a sort of
scruple as to the length of his letters to his family.
His cell was his delight, and he realized the promises

in the "Imitation" to those who jealously guard their little sanctuary.

"Everything speaks to me in my cell," he writes to his sister. "I love it as a mother loves her child. Everything about it encourages me to charity and devotion. I come in; to the right is my holy water stoup, and it seems to say to me, 'Your cell is your sanctuary; nothing impure must enter it,' and so I leave my worldliness at the door, and purify myself with holy water. I walk towards the window and look out on the sky, and I say to myself, 'Up there a place is reserved for you; work and struggle hard to win it.' Then I beg of our Lord to bless my labor, and lest any strange thought should disturb my mind, there hangs my Crucifix, preaching forever by the Divine example. Then above my book-case, the Cross stretches out its arms and covers me with its shadow; and soon I shall have also the picture of Mary Immaculate watching over her Child. You fancy that I may have some troubles in my present life, dear Mélanie? No; I do assure you this place is to me a paradise upon earth. Everyone is happy here, even those who, like me, are far from being saints!"

At the same time he was ever mindful of his home ties, and seized every little opportunity for opening his heart to his family. "How good you are to me!" he wrote one day, "and how I love you for your tender thought of me! I said, 'I want some sleeves,' and in a trice here they are! 'I should like a curtain for my window,' and there it hangs, keeping out all curious eyes. I desired some money, and behold, here it is, without my asking! as well as half a dozen minor things which make my little establishment complete. Only one thing is lacking and that is time! A little quarter of an hour to say, 'Thank you!' and again 'Thank you!'"

On one occasion he describes to his family the departure of one of the seminarians for the foreign missions, and his secret wish for the first time breaks forth: "Several vocations of the like nature have declared themselves," he exclaims. "It is quite glorious! We are in a state of excitement and enthusiasm about it not to be described." These words awoke some fears at home, especially in the heart of the sister who knew him best; and he writes in reply, "So my news troubled you, dear little sister, did it? But is there anything so very extraordinary in the fact that one among us is going to devote himself to the salvation of the heathen? Why, one talks of going to be a Jesuit; another, to La Trappe; another to China; and so on! Oh, if you think there are no events and no gossip in the Seminary, you are very much mistaken. But you have created a whole world of hope and fears out of that one little sentence of mine! I can scarcely help laughing. Another time don't let your imagination run wild, but sleep in peace."

In this humble and hidden life, like that of his Master at Nazareth, nothing is so striking as the way he passed from the natural to the supernatural. Everything spoke to him of God. One day after telling his brother how at Easter he had changed his room, and altered the arrangement of his things, he adds, "It is quite an event for me, this change; and now I am going to work away with fresh courage, for one thought pursues me, and seems to me to be at the bottom of all my college life.

"Why have I come here? *Ad quid venisti?* Why come to a theological seminary? It is to go through a certain course of instruction, you will say. Well, but that course comes to an end; *and then?* . . . Oh, when that thought comes to me, I can simply bow my head, and beg God to answer me. I will do as He shall appoint."

The ceremonies and anniversaries of the Church as celebrated in the Seminary impressed him strongly, and were the constant subjects of his letters. On Good Friday he was especially moved, and wrote as follows:—

"Oh, this is indeed a sad and exceptional day at the Seminary! . . . To see us all mournfully wandering here and there in the cloisters, without a sound being heard, not a voice, not even a whisper, one would imagine we were sheep without a shepherd. And it is quite true; the Pastor of pastors is dead; the Pastor has given His life for His sheep."

These thoughts, which seemed to come naturally to the young theological student, were often poured out to his brother and sister. With his younger brother, especially, it seemed to him the best and most delicate way of making him take an interest in serious things without disgusting him by lectures, or appearing to be always "preaching" to him. "I like to think of you on these occasions," he wrote one day, "and I fancy I see you, so recollected in prayer, so studious in class, so merry and gay at recreation, and making us all so glad and happy! for to be good is to be happy; and we cannot be thoroughly happy unless you are the same."

In the faithful practice of all these relative duties, Theophane made the best preparation for the priest-hood. The Christmas ordination, at which he had only assisted as a spectator, had touched him to the quick. When that of Trinity came around, he was told to prepare himself for the first step by receiving the tonsure.

"My dearest Sister," he writes, "to-morrow I am to be tonsured; that is, I shall no longer belong to the world, but to our Lord. I shall say to Him, 'My God, Thou art the portion of my heritage, and of my lot. Thou wilt give me a place in Thy Heavenly Kingdom.' I shall say to the Blessed Virgin, *'Regina cleri, ora pro nobis!'*† Oh how proud I shall be to wear on my head the crown of the saints! that crown to obtain which it would not be too much to devote one's whole life!"

But his happiness was to be delayed some time, owing to the death of the beloved bishop of the diocese. In so public a calamity his generous soul could not think for a moment of a personal disappointment which had been swallowed up in the general mourning. Just before the long vacation his father's feast day occurred; and in spite of the press of work before the examinations, he found time to write a few loving words: "My dearest Father,—I try to fancy myself with you on Saturday evening, and embrace you with all my heart, while offering you the flower which most expresses my humble but devoted love. O Thou who art the Master of life and death, preserve to us our darling father; watch over him, and keep him in all his ways now and ever."

The first year of his seminary life was over, and it had been fruitful in gifts and graces. But always afraid of himself, and fearful lest he should relax during the long vacation, he wrote out a series of resolutions, which we will give verbatim:—

---

†Queen of the Clergy, pray for us.

July 1, 1849.

A. M. D. G.

SOME RESOLUTIONS FOR THE HOLIDAYS.

One year of my seminary life is already past, and I must give an account of this time of retreat and sanctification. Alas! where are the graces which I have acquired? My God, Thou hast searched me out, and known me. Even the angels are not pure in Thy sight; and what am I? . . . O my divine Redeemer, have mercy upon me. Deign to accept my penitence, and to bless the resolutions which, with the help of Thy grace, I hope to make for the future. Virgin Mother! thou whom from my childhood I have chosen, pray for me, for thou art my refuge and my strength. *"Refugium peccatorum, ora pro nobis!"*†

1. I will get up the moment I wake, offering my heart to Jesus and Mary. I will never sleep later than six. If I serve the six o'clock Mass, I will say my prayers and the "little hours" afterwards; if the eight o'clock, then I will say them all before, together with my meditation and the study of a certain portion of Holy Scripture. The rest of the Office I will say in the evening at separate times.

2. I will make a particular examen every day before luncheon at two o'clock. This examination is to consist of a few minutes' meditation on faith, charity, modesty, interior recollection, etc., etc., with a special consideration of the way in which I have practised each. At the end of the month I will make a general examination, to prevent my relapsing into laxity or indifference.

3. In the course of the afternoon or evening I will

---

† Refuge of Sinners, pray for us.

visit the Blessed Sacrament, making use of St. Alphonsus Liguori's Exercises on the subject. I will also take for my meditation book the *"Memoriale Vitae Sacerdotalis"* (by Claude Arvisenet), besides the "Imitation" and the Holy Scriptures, both of which I always carry with me.

4. Directly after breakfast I will spend an hour or so in working either at my holiday task or at the Holy Scriptures. In the evening, after Vespers and Compline, I will study again a little bit, but on less serious subjects. I could do this while walking, or when I am waiting at the Curé's.

5. In my intercourse with the outside world, I will try to be most careful in speech. I will be gentle and kind toward everyone, and especially towards my own family. Should the occasion present itself, I will never neglect to say a little word of our good God, especially to children. But I will do this with great caution, remembering that deeds are worth more than words.

6. On feast days I will work between Mass and Vespers if I have time. On those days I will try to keep up a greater spirit of recollection.

7. Of these resolutions, there are a few which I must strictly put into practice; such are those in regard to prayer, the particular examen, the visit to the Blessed Sacrament, and the spiritual reading of the "Imitation" or the "Memoriale."

As to the other points I may be less severe, especially if my friends or companions insist upon my accompanying them on a walk or on a party of pleasure. In fact, I must be careful to do nothing singular or out of the way, so as to excite observation; all affectation, therefore, is *tabooed*. True merit is hidden and simple, and dreads nothing more than publicity. If

I can only keep always humble, charitable, and modest, I may escape some of the dangers of my long vacation. I am sure good examples will not be wanting to me; and then, have I not the grace of God? *"Dominus custodiat te. Dominus protectio tua. Omnia possum in eo qui me confortat."†*

T. Vénard.

In this little rule of life no mention is made of the frequentation of the Sacraments or other devotions; but as he followed strictly the rule of the Seminary in all these points, it was not necessary to speak of them. No mention is made either of the rosary. It was said every evening in his family circle, and Theophane presided at it during his holidays as a matter of course. Some readers may be surprised at the simplicity of this rule and its few austerities. This arose from his determination to keep it strictly, so that it should not be a dead letter. Moreover, he thought it right for the sake of those around him to share in their simple pleasures, and in the expeditions and picnics which took place during his visit. His greatest delight was to be with his sister, and to talk with her of holy things and of their future vocations; and daily was the soul of each strengthened by their mutual intercourse.

Two months after his return to the Seminary (on the 8th of December), Mgr. Pie, the new Bishop of Poitiers, made his solemn entry into his episcopal town. The sight of this young and saintlike Bishop had a great effect on Theophane, all the more so as it ensured the Christmas ordination, when he was to receive the tonsure. From that moment he considered himself as set apart for the priesthood, and re-

†May the Lord keep thee. The Lord is thy protector. I can do all things in Him who strengtheneth me.

doubled his zeal and fervor. At the Trinity ordination, in 1850, he received minor orders, and wrote to
his father, "Oh what a grand day is that of one's ordination! How I wish you had been here to share in
my joy! But you will come, will you not, when the
great and final step is taken? You will add your blessing to the rest? Oh, it seems as if I could hardly wait
patiently for the dawning of such a great day!"

The vacation came round again, and Theophane
took the opportunity to open his heart more entirely to
his sister, both for his own consolation and because he
knew that her faith would triumph over all human
considerations, and help him to overcome the shrink-
ings of his loving heart as he thought over a separation
which would probably be final. He spent almost the
whole time at home, and employed part of it in helping his brother to make a little grass terrace at the foot
of the garden,* where, he fancied, after his departure
they would be able to sit and think of the absent
one whom they had freely given for God's work. On
his return to the Seminary he seems to have redoubled
his efforts to profit by this last year of study and
preparation for his future career. But he did not neglect others in thinking of himself, and his letters to
his little brother and to his sister are more frequent
than ever. To the former he writes on the beauty of
piety in the young, adding, however, "Now don't imagine it necessary to put on a sour face, or to look
sanctimonious. True devotion is natural, gay, and

---

*The Vénard home at St. Loup was in possession of the family until
the death of Fr. Eusebius in 1913. According to the custom of
the country, a high stone-wall encloses the long, narrow garden in
the rear, where Fr. Eusebius pointed out to the writer, on one of
his visits, vegetable beds, rose-trees and lilies,—the many fruits of
Theophane's vacation labors. [Ed.

bright, according to the words of St. Paul, '*Gaudete in Domino semper; iterum dico, gaudete.*' "†

To his sister he writes more as to an equal.

"I rejoice, my darling Mélanie, to see you growing every day in fervor and the love of God. I am sure we shall both try not to forget that humility is the base of all perfection, and that obedience is its guardian. Read Rodriguez's article on Humility in his work on Christian Perfection. But do not let this book give you any scruples, as it is addressed to nuns, and one must not confound absolute precepts with practices which vary according to the position and duties of each person. . . . I quite understand what you say in your letters about the sacrifice hanging over our heads. Courage! God asks of us only our good will; His grace does the rest. What I am most afraid of, is lest you should be discouraged. The Christian motto is Hope! Hope on! hope ever! Be very generous to our good God. Try to leave all things to Him, without trouble or preoccupation. 'In quietness and confidence shall be your strength.' If you feel you have been wanting in such sentiments, make a little act of contrition, and then rise again quickly with renewed courage. In this way we shall really feel as children of God in the holy liberty wherewith Christ has made us free. To be truly humble; to fly from this world's notice; to hold ourselves continually as in the presence of God; to be little in our own eyes,—these are the dispositions which are most pleasing to Him, and which are easier for you to practise than for many others, on account of your quiet, hidden life, very like that of the Holy Family of Nazareth. . . . A great

---

†Rejoice in the Lord always; again I say, rejoice.

step must soon be taken—the sub-diaconate—a step for
life and for eternity! Oh, pray for me, that I may
in all things follow God's will, and that I may fully
know what He requires of me. Say the 'Memorare'
frequently for me with this intention. You know
how I thank and love you beforehand for all that you
do for me in that and a thousand other ways."

To his father he writes, in view of his approaching
vows:

"I am now at an age when my future career must
be decided upon, and perhaps there may be a question of my marriage. All this might have been a subject of great anxiety and trouble to you. But, my
dearest father, I have chosen my own path. Do not
seek an earthly partner for me. Our Lord has called
me, utterly unworthy as I am. He has asked for my
whole heart, for my body, soul, and spirit, and can I
refuse Him what is His? And then I turn in thought
to you, from whom, next to God, I have received all—
to you, my darling father, and I ask, do not you wish
the same thing for me? Are you not willing to give
me up to God? *To give me up without reserve; to
make a complete sacrifice of your child?* Oh, I am
sure you will say yes! For if you have a father's
heart, you have equally the heart of a fervent, loving
Catholic. . . . But I would add one word more. Is
it not the father who takes the bride to the house of
God, who gives her to her spouse? Do not her friends
and relatives accompany her? Oh, I am sure you will
do the same by me! You will come to this my marriage, the mysterious union which joins a human soul
to its Creator. You will come to offer to God the
child He has given you. You will come and bless me
not only in your own name, but in that of her who I

feel sure is now helping us with her prayers before the Throne of God. You will bless me for my mother."

We add to this touching letter the few words he addressed to his godmother on the same occasion:— "I hasten to tell you a piece of news. Perhaps my dear godmother has forgotten that the little child she carried to the Baptismal Font is now twenty-one, the age required by the Church for the office of sub-deacon. Well, I have made up my mind, or rather it is not I that have settled it, but God who has chosen one so miserable and unworthy as I to serve at His altar. And can I say 'No'? I can only adore the mercy of God, and nature must submit. So, on the 21st of this month I am to be ordained sub-deacon. My father, I trust, will come to the sacrifice of his son; but I have no mother left on earth. Dare I ask my godmother—my mother in the order of grace—to take her place?"

The day of immolation came, and the sacrifice was consummated. Then the young sub-deacon sought his Director with the words, "Now I am ready—you will no longer oppose my wish? you will let me go?" And the good and prudent Director assented, and at once wrote to Paris to obtain his admittance to the Foreign Mission Seminary. His much-loved sister and little brother were unable to be present at his ordination; but to console them he wrote the following words:—

"Dearest Mélanie,—Your brother is at last a sub-deacon! My soul overflows with joy, but with a joy so sweet and so pure that I cannot express it. I should like to be able to tell you all I feel, but I cannot put it

into words. I took the terrible step without trembling.
God, in His infinite goodness, spared me the agony of
fear at the moment. My knees did not knock against
each other, nor did my foot fail me. When I was
stretched on the pavement I was filled only with a solemn calm; but when I got up I felt as if I had broken
every link, as if I were for the first time free—free
like a little bird who has escaped from the snare of the
fowler. Oh, how willingly would I then have flown
up to heaven!"

To his brother he writes more gaily:—

"MY DEAR LITTLE EUSEBIUS,—Henry IV. said,
'Hang thyself, brave Crillon! we have won a victory,
and thou wert not there!' I shall say, too, 'You were
not there when your poor old brother, prostrate on
the pavement, gave himself irrevocably to God!' But
I know well that it was not your fault. Therefore
please do not hang yourself! but help me to thank our
dear Lord for the great grace He has bestowed upon
me, and for the happiness with which I am filled.
Gratias Deo super inenarrabili dono ejus! † Oh, it
was a great day, and a day that has no ending—*quae
nescit occasum diei!* Its dawn will be brighter and
brighter until we come to eternity. And now, my
dearest little brother, I feel as if I had acquired a right
to say to you, 'Do not love the world or its pleasures.'
They are seemingly attractive and beautiful; but
within all is corruption, vileness, emptiness, and remorse. O my brother, let us love God, our dear, good
God, and be as sheep under His hand! Love Him, and
you will have no cause for repentance even on this

---

†Thanks be to God for his unspeakable gift!

earth. He, too, promises us joys and pleasures, but they are joys certain, inexpressible, eternal,—*pax Dei quae exsuperat omnem sensum!*"†

The answer soon came from Paris, and it was favorable. Then the young student began to make his preparations to leave the Poitiers Seminary, bid adieu to his family, and start joyfully for that house which for more than two centuries has trained Apostles for Eastern Asia.

---

†The peace of God which surpasseth all understanding.

3

CHAPTER IV.

Breaking Home Ties.

THEOPHANE'S departure for the Paris Seminary was definitely settled, and it became necessary to break the news to his family, and especially to his father, who, proud of his son, had already made endless plans for his future advancement.   Theophane knew this; and although he thoroughly appreciated his father's courage and generosity, he yet shrunk, as his favorite child, from inflicting a blow which, he well knew, would annihilate all his father's hopes. Nevertheless, he could not bear that a strange hand should give the tidings, and so he summoned courage to pen the following letter, which we give in its entirety.

"February 7, 1851.

"MY DEAREST FATHER,—It is a little more than a month ago that, to my great joy, you came to witness my consecration to the service of God. You yourself, as it were, presented the victim at the altar. A poor and miserable offering indeed! yet such as it was our Lord in His infinite mercy accepted it. And since that moment how the time has flown! God guides the hearts of men, and they follow as He leads. God, as it were, took me by the hand, and spoke to me with an irresistible voice. 'My son!' He said, 'come, follow Me, fear nothing; you are little, and poor, and weak, and miserable, but I am the Almighty God. Come, I will be with thee!' And I, can I have a will in presence of the will of God?

"My dearly-loved father, have you understood me? One day God said to Abraham, 'Take thy only-begotten son, Isaac, whom thou lovest, and go into the land of Vision; and there thou shalt offer him for a holocaust upon one of the mountains which I shall show thee.' And Abraham obeyed without a moment's hesitation, and without a murmur; and his obedience was most pleasing to God. Now, my dearest father, do you begin to understand me? Here am I, the child whom you love; I have not borrowed a strange pen to tell you the truth. I come openly, without any subterfuges unworthy of us both. God calls me; yes, it is His call. Oh, call me likewise; say that you, too, are willing that your Theophane should become a missioner!

"Poor father! the word is said,—the *Foreign Missions*. Do not let your human nature shrink from the thought. Rather kneel and take your crucifix, that crucifix which received my mother's last breath, and say, 'My God, I consent, may Thy holy will be done. Amen.'

"O my father, forgive me for having struck the blow myself! Some people will tell you I am mad, ungrateful, a bad son, and I know not what besides. My darling father, you will not think so! I know you have a great and generous soul, and one that has drunk deeply at the only true source of real strength and greatness—that of Religion and Faith. I have saddened your heart; my own is sorrowful and heavy too. The sacrifice asked of us is hard—most hard! But, O Lord Jesus! since Thou dost will it, I will it likewise, and so willeth my father.

"Courage, then, my dearest father—courage, and

resignation and confidence in God and in His Holy
Mother. Let us pray for each other. Father, I kneel
at your feet. Bless your child, and believe in his respectful devotion and dutiful submission.

Theophane Vénard, Sub-deacon."

As he knew beforehand, this letter came upon his
father as a thunder-clap; nevertheless the blow did not
leave a sting behind, for M. Vénard was a large-
hearted and generous Catholic. His answer, which we
subjoin, was one of consent, and a consent so heartily
given that it rivalled the sublime virtue of his son.
One day, when a friend was trying to console M.
Vénard by assuring him that his son's vocation had
been abundantly weighed and proved by his superiors
before they gave their assent, he exclaimed, "And
what would become of the prophecy of our Lord Jesus
Christ, who declared that His Gospel should be
preached throughout the whole earth, if directors of
colleges and heads of families were to check the aspirations of all the young students who wish to embark for the foreign missions?"

Such was the frank, loyal, generous nature of the
father of the future missioner, and his character is
well shown in the following letter:—

"St. Loup, *February* 12, 1851.

"MY DEAREST, WELL-BELOVED SON,—I will not attempt to describe the emotion your letter caused me.
I fancy you had calculated beforehand the force of
the blow. You may well say that the sacrifice is hard.
Your ordination cost me nothing. On the contrary, it
fulfilled my fondest wishes for you, and I was quite
content. But now everything is changed. All my
plans are upset. Well may people say, 'Man proposes,

ST. LOUP,
The Birthplace of Theophane Vénard.

and God disposes.' I had flattered myself that you would some day have a parish near me, that I should be able to make over everything to Henry, and then come and finish my days quietly under your roof, so that you should close my eyes. Happy, but, alas! hopeless illusions.

"My child, I cannot attempt to try to turn you from your great and holy resolutions. Neither will I sadden your heart by reproaches. I will content myself with asking if, at your age, you think you can really arrive at so serious a decision, and not regret it hereafter. But if you are resolved, if you feel that God has indeed called you, then I would say, 'Obey Him without hesitation.' Let nothing keep you back, not even the thought of the poor old father whom you leave in his sorrowful desolation, nor of the paternal roof which will no longer shelter you. Enough; I know that he who puts his hand to the plough must not look behind him; I know also that he who leaves father and mother to follow his Lord will receive an eternal recompense, and such reasons are unanswerable. . . . I could not reply to your letter at once, my dearest son, for poor human nature would have its way at first. But to-day I am a little calmer, and I hasten to fulfil your wishes. You ask for my consent. I give it to you without restriction. My blessing—O my dearest boy, why should I refuse it to you? You know that I belong only to my children, and that you may always reckon on me. All that gives you pleasure gives it to me likewise, cost what it will. My sacrifices began when you first went to school and I was separated from you; they went on increasing year by year, and now God knows where they are to end! Well, I can only resign myself and leave all in the hands of Him who, perhaps, will give me back my Isaac, as you have compared me to the Father of the Faithful.

"Do not let my letter sadden you too much. I cannot put my ideas down as I wish, but you will guess my thoughts. Let us hope that God will sustain us both in this great trial. Although your sister knew of your intention beforehand, she was terribly affected by your declaration, for she flattered herself the day was still far off. But, as you say, the time is short. . . . Henry saw at once that there was something the matter but I have told him nothing as yet. And poor little Eusebius, whom you were to mould and form, is he to lose his model and his guide? Forgive my saying this—forgive your poor old father, who lives but in his children. I feel I have gone too far, and that I shall give you pain, and you don't deserve it.

"Bear in mind, then, that I freely give my consent to your plans. Be at peace, and do not trouble about me. The hand of God is everywhere. I love you with all my heart and embrace you tenderly.

Vénard."

So the future missioner could go to the Foreign Mission Seminary without fear, and instead of the anger of his father, he was to meet with nothing but love and blessings. Theophane's feelings found vent in the following letter to his sister:—

"MY DARLING SISTER,—Oh, how I cried when I read your letter! Yes, I knew well the sorrow I was going to bring upon my family, and especially upon you, my dear little sister. But don't you think it cost me tears of blood, too, to take such a step, and give you all such pain? Who ever cared more for home and a home life than I? All my happiness here below was centred in

it. But God, who has united us all in links of the
tenderest affection, wished to wean me from it. Oh,
what a fight and a struggle I have had with my poor
human nature! But then our Lord, who asked the
sacrifice at my hands, gave me the strength to accomplish it. He did more. He gave me the courage to
offer myself the bitter chalice to those I loved. I undertook it because I knew you all so well, and I was
full of faith and hope; and that hope has not been disappointed. And now I can only adore His mercy, and
praise Him who has led me so tenderly through this
terrible trial.

"Can it be, then, that family ties and family joys
are not holy and blessed? Has God forbidden them?
Or were our hearts too absorbed in them, so that God,
to punish us, wished to withdraw them altogether? Or
have we all gone crazy? No! no! a thousand times no!
Let the world say what it will. What matters it to us,
children of grace, who have received the heavenly
promises? The world and its maxims have long ago
had their condemnation from the mouth of our Divine
Lord Himself. Ah! Lord God, Thy thoughts are not
as our thoughts, and Thou walkest by paths of which
the world knows nothing.

"See, my dearest sister, how He has led us until
now. We had a good and darling mother, and she
was taken from us just as we were entering upon
life. How we have cried for her! But God took pity
on her children. He has given you strength and wisdom to take her place in the family. Then another
sacrifice was asked of us. You, my good little sister,
had long given yourself to God. You wanted to do
so altogether, but Providence contented itself with
your will and your submission, and did not exact the
consummation of the sacrifice. But God was watch-

ing over your poor brother. He was conducting him
as by the hand in a path traced out by Himself. Oh,
miracle of grace! Oh, the depth and the riches of the
goodness and mercy of God! He who needs not human instruments to accomplish His great designs,
chooses the vilest, the most miserable of His creatures
to do His work. I, wretched little I, receive the mission and the inspiration of the Apostolate. . . . Dearest sister, say with me that our God is good—infinitely
good. Let all the earth echo the words and repeat
them in a transport of gratitude and joy. See how our
Lord loves us. See how He showers His gifts upon
us. One more sacrifice is asked of us; but does not
our Lord prove those He loves so as to make them
more worthy of Himself? Must we not all pass
through the crucible? A cross is given to us. Let us
embrace it generously, and thank Him. Our tears
must flow. Well, let us offer them up to Him who has
called them forth. This earth is after all but a valley
of tears; and the Divine Master has said, 'Blessed are
those that mourn, for they shall be comforted.' And
then, even if we do part here for a little time, it is only
our bodies that are separated. Our souls are united
more closely than ever in thoughts which know no
space or distance. We shall meet one another in
heaven. Yes, all of us shall be together then. Let us
trust in God, and make the sacrifice generously. And
then you have Henry; and God will watch over poor
little Eusebius. Let us pray and trust and hope, and
remain united to each other in the hearts of Jesus and
Mary. . . And now I must add a line to my dear
father. You don't know how proud I am to be his son!
I long to feel myself in his arms, pressed to his heart.
. . . My father, with your great courage, firm faith,
burning love—all for God—even your Theophane!

Dearest father, these souls that I am going to strive to win for our Lord, I offer them all to you, next to God. They will be your crown and your glory in the Home of the Elect.

"I am going away, but I leave you an angel of consolation—a loving guardian angel—in Mélanie. When the time of your pilgrimage is over, Mélanie will close your eyes, will pray by your bedside, and will speak to you of your poor little missioner; and you will bless her and him too. But why do I speak of death? Oh, please God, you will live many, many years yet to be the joy and the providence of your children! The little missioner will get letters from you from time to time, and news of all the family, and that will be a great joy to him. I hope also to spend a *good long fortnight* with my dear ones at home and enjoy them thoroughly before I start."

The "little missioner" accordingly went home on Saturday, the 15th of February. He arranged to walk from Parthenay, so as to meet his brother Henry and have a talk with him before they saw their father. The only idea of something extraordinary about to happen was from a little note which Theophane had written to both his brothers in these words: "I implore you to say the 'Memorare' for me every day till we meet, that I may obtain a great grace. You will soon know why." But the poor children were far from guessing the truth.

Henry, being then eighteen, at once understood the gravity and importance of the step which his brother was about to take. As for poor little Eusebius, his uncertainty came to an end the next day when Theophane called to carry him off for a fortnight from his studies. He had set his heart on having the whole family together on this occasion, so as to enjoy for the last time the happiness which such a home circle alone can give.

It is easy to understand how trying these last few days were to them all; but to Theophane they were the hardest. He had to be tender, affectionate, and loving to every one, and yet firm and determined in his resolution to leave them. At times he could scarcely contain himself, and he had to do incessant violence to his own heart to maintain any kind of decent calm. But he acquitted himself marvellously.

We cannot attempt to describe his first meeting with his father. They embraced each other closely in silence, without tears or sighs. Only after a time the words, "My dearest boy!" "My good father!" burst from the lips of each. These few words said all to those who could feel and understand what was passing in two such loving hearts.

These touching scenes were renewed very often in the course of the trying fortnight, especially towards evening, near the fireside after dinner, when there would often be a dead silence, the father contenting himself with pressing his son's hand and not daring to trust himself to speak. The future missioner would try to cheer them all by droll stories, or interest them in the countries he was so soon to visit. At last he excited them so much on the subject of China and the missions, that nothing would content Mélanie and her brothers but the thought of going too. They made a thousand little plans, in which each was to share in his labors. "And what is to become of me?" at last exclaimed their father, who had been silently listening to their fine projects. "Am I to be left like poor old Zebedee to mend my nets? Rather than that,

I will go too." Indeed he several times told his son that nothing but his duty to his other children kept him back, adding that he had no longer anything else to bind him, and that all he asked of God was to be allowed time to launch his children in life, and then sing his "Nunc Dimittis."

So the days sped on, only too rapidly, and each evening became more sad as it grew nearer to the one which was to hear the last farewell. Poor Mélanie felt the strain especially, and every night would linger after the others to get the last kiss and the last word. There was always something more to say and the last night of all they made no attempt to retire. Mélanie had several little things to add to his outfit; and he sat watching her, saying as many loving things as his sad heart would allow. Ten years later, Theophane, then a Confessor for the Faith, remembered every single incident of that night, which consoled him even in the bottom of his cage. Only two days before his martyrdom, he wrote to his sister, "It was alone with you that I passed that delicious night of the 26th of February, 1851, that night at home which was the scene of our last interview on earth, spent in holy, helpful, consoling talk like that of St. Benedict and his sister."

The day of departure came at last. The whole family sought strength where alone it could be found, and received Holy Communion together. Theophane served the Mass with a rapt manner and expression, which made him look more like an angel than a man. Then came farewell visits to friends and relatives, when he tried to turn aside sorrowful thoughts and anticipations by a bright, gay manner, and occasional little jokes; yet he owned afterwards that he was nearly suffocated with sorrow. One visit cost

him many tears,—it was to the churchyard, to the
tomb of his mother, whom he had so idolized, and from
whom he had been separated at the hour of her death,
so that he had never had her dying blessing—to him a
cause of eternal regret. He could scarcely tear himself away from those precious remains. And yet the
thought of this visit was most consoling to him afterwards, and he always spoke of it with tears of gratitude.

The hour of departure was fixed for nine o'clock in
the evening. Theophane had chosen that time to
avoid a crowd of anxious and sympathizing friends;
his brother and one old friend were to drive him to
Parthenay, where he would take the night train. The
family sat down to dinner earlier than usual, the good
old pastor of the village having joined them; and Theophane, by almost superhuman efforts, succeeded in
making the meal cheerful, almost gay. But a few
words from his father towards the end brought back
sad and sorrowful thoughts, and they all became more
and more silent. The dinner was over and the time
of departure was drawing nearer every moment. As
usual they said the rosary together, then read a chapter from the Imitation, after which they knelt for
evening prayers. No one had the courage to lead
except Theophane himself, and as he went on the
sobs and tears of his little audience became more
pronounced. Whatever restraint we may put upon our
feelings before men, the barrier breaks down when we
find ourselves alone with God! Theophane with difficulty finished the prayer, and approaching his father,
said, "The hour is come; we must part. My father,
will you not bless your son, your poor little Theophane?" As he spoke, he threw himself at his father's
feet, embracing his knees. The poor father lifted his

eyes and his hands to Heaven, and with a broken voice, making the sign of the Cross on his child's head, said, "My dearest son, receive the blessing of your father, who offers you a willing sacrifice to our Lord. May you be blessed forever and forever, in the name of the Father, and of the Son, and of the Holy Ghost. Amen!"

Then Theophane rising, knelt for a moment in the same way for the good old priest's blessing, and rapidly kissed his whole family, as he did each evening before going to bed; but this was for the last time! Henry went out to see if the carriage was ready. Eusebius threw himself into his brother's arms, sobbing as if his little heart would break. Mélanie, kissing him and crying "Only once more," fell back almost fainting on her chair. The poor father, still and immovable from excess of sorrow, leaned heavily on the arm of his old friend, the Curé.

"Courage! let us be generous in our sacrifices!" murmured the poor missioner. He could bear no more. With one last kiss to his half-unconscious sister, he seized his cloak and hat, and rushed into the carriage. Then several friends and townspeople crowded round him, to shake hands for the last time. He wrung their hands, exclaiming "Good-bye! good-bye! we shall meet in our true home," and the carriage set off rapidly for Parthenay. The sacrifice was over, and M. Vénard, without wronging his other children, could say, "I have lost the fairest flower in my garden!" The delay at the moment of departure, though slight, made them miss the train at Parthenay by five minutes. This was a minor but very real trial to our poor Theophane, who longed for the final parting to be over. But there was no help for it, and so Theophane and Henry waited for the next train, which

started at six o'clock in the morning. His brother
remarked that when once settled in the railway carriage, Theophane looked away, and burying his face
in his hands, cried bitterly and uncontrollably, to re-
lieve the poor heart which had with such difficulty
contained itself during the long ordeal.*

---

*Henry, who was alive when the writer first visited Assai, remembered
this night vividly. He died shortly before the Beatification. [Ed.

CHAPTER V.

In Paris—The "Missions Étrangères."

THREE days after the sad parting we have just recorded, Theophane left Poitiers for Paris, and arrived at the Foreign Mission Seminary. "I had hardly come into the house," he wrote to his sister, "when I was met with affectionate greetings on all sides, and every kindness was showered upon me. One hoisted up my trunk into my cell; another uncorded it; a third made my bed and showed me where my little establishment was to be; a fourth took me all over the house, introduced me to the Directors, and showed me the garden. In half an hour I felt as if I knew them all intimately. Oh, the good their welcome did to my poor, sad heart! There is nothing like the love and charity of this house and the way they make one feel immediately at home."

This spirit of charity and mutual kindness is the distinguishing characteristic of the Foreign Mission Seminary in Paris. Its divine fire is carefully maintained by the superiors as the best means of spreading its genial rays to the extremities of the heathen world. In the heart of a great city, and in a world gone drunk with dissipation and all kinds of business, these young men find an abode of peace and quiet indeed, but no ascetic solitude. Rather is it a home where each strives to be foremost in loving, kindly ways and con-

sideration for the others; and the Holy Spirit seems
especially to bless this atmosphere of mutual charity
and forbearance, and to pour His sevenfold gifts on
the future Apostles, who are learning in that best of
schools—for it is our Lord's—the school of love.*

Theophane was thoroughly happy here, although
his new life did not altogether do away with the
bitterness of separation from those he held most dear.

He writes, "We are all like one family, with one
object and one aim. We have no care or troubles and
I should have nothing left to desire if you were by
my side. I am greatly touched by your anxiety about
me, my dearest father, but you must let me scold you
about this a little bit. Am I not more than ever the
child of Providence? Did you not yourself give me up
to God? He who watches over the birds of the air
and the flowers of the field, will He not take care of
me wherever I may be? I cannot help longing for you,
and missing you terribly sometimes; but love suffers
and is resigned, and the thoughts of Heaven grow
more vivid as we become more detached from all on
earth. Only a little more trust! A little more confidence in God! A little more patience! and the end will
come, and the past weary years will seem as nothing;
then will arrive the moment of reunion, and all will
be amply compensated for and repaid, principal and
interest. O Christian hope! How beautiful thou art!

---

*The writer has been privileged to remain as a guest at the Missions
Étrangères in Paris. The atmosphere of this house is indescribable.
One feels about him the presence of a purely unselfish love of God.
The recreations are full of life, the students at times even boisterous,
though never rough; sadness finds no resting place on the features
of these bright young men who are preparing to be apostles, perhaps
martyrs. Any consciousness of the spirit of self-sacrifice, which to
an eminent degree they all possess, is entirely lacking. On the
contrary, humility expresses itself so naturally in their words and
acts, that one dwelling among these chosen souls hardly realizes the
heroism of purpose and the burning love with which they are ani-
mated. [Ed.

PARIS SEMINARY FOR FOREIGN MISSIONS.
The Chapel.

How thou dost satisfy the heart of man, the creature of a day, and yet created for an eternity of bliss!"

His family could not rise at once to his spiritual view of the future, and their letters gave evidence of the void he had left behind and their despair at losing him. His answers, therefore, were written at this time to heal the wound he had caused, and he had always a kind and loving word for the consolation of each. To Henry he writes, "Your letter touched me deeply, especially where you say that the thought of me is not enough—that you want my *bodily* presence to comfort you. I feel just the same about you all. My thoughts fly home to the little room where you all are in the evening, and to my place by Mélanie's side, and to the thousand and one recollections of our boyhood. But it is God's Will that we should be separated. May that Will be forever blessed! After all, are we not bound for the same haven? Will not the gaps in the family circle then be filled up? Nay, more, are we not already expected *up there* by one most near and dear to us? You recollect our last visit before leaving home—the visit paid at your suggestion—to the cemetery, where we prayed and cried so together for our darling mother? Well, very soon we shall go and join her; and the links that bind us are tightened at the thought, and the time which seems *so long* and *weary* is bridged over."

To his sister he says, "If I have read your dear letter over once, I have read it twenty times! Every word you say goes to my heart, for we are *one*—are we not? —with the same feelings, the same tastes, the same wishes, the same hopes. We really are, as the saying is, born for each other; and how comes it, then, that we are separated? Why, because God wished that

4

we should be united eternally. As you said yourself one day, dearest Mélanie, if we could live together here below, we should have cared too much for the world, and so He has divided us that our souls may be more and more purified, and sigh more and more after the moment when they shall take their flight to Heaven. A great servant of God once said that 'if some gall were not mingled in our earthly cup, we should be content with our exile, and think less of our own true country.' . . ."

To Eusebius he sends also a word of loving sympathy: "You cannot imagine the pleasure your letters have given me. I know well my poor little brother's tender, loving heart, but I rejoice that you have struggled against your sorrow, and not given way to it too much. You have thrown yourself into Mary's arms as a child into the arms of its mother. What a comfort it is to be able to do that in our moments of loneliness and desolation! Let Mary always be your refuge, my darling brother. The Blessed Virgin is much loved and honored in the Mission House here. When you have any little sorrow or trouble go simply to her, and ask her to offer it up for you to our dear Lord, and there leave it without any further care or preoccupation. Then you will have nothing to fear either from men or devils. You will walk quietly in the path of life until you come hopefully to that home for which we all sigh and where we wish to be!"

After what we have told our readers, it is not to be wondered at that Theophane not only won all hearts at the Seminary, but made rapid progress in the paths of perfection. His humility and simplicity concealed **even from** himself the beauty of his soul, but it could

not be hidden from his superiors, and still less from his
holy and wise director. Among the students, two,
M. Dallet and M. Theurel, soon won a high place
in his affections.* But fearful lest the tie should
become too human, they mutually agreed to tell each
other their faults, and so to make their very intimacy
a means of advancing more rapidly in their heaven-
bound path. Theophane fulfilled this compact consci-
entiously, and it might have been thought almost se-
verely, if his words had not been tempered by such
extreme humility and sweetness as to disarm all
inclination to wounded feeling. As far as he himself
was concerned, he was his own severest accuser, and
often his humility led him to exaggerate his short-
comings to such an extent that he honestly believed
himself utterly unfit for the apostolic life he had
chosen and besought the prayers of all his friends
for his conversion. He even had himself publicly
recommended at Notre Dame des Victoires, and, writing to a lady who had been preparing various little
things for his future chapel, he says, "I am not sure of
being allowed to go. I feel myself so utterly unworthy! Not that my desire is altered; on the contrary, I am more firmly resolved than ever. But the
decision does not rest with me. May His holy will
be done! After all, if they think me unworthy of
the missionary life, you must not be troubled; for it
is not for me you have been working, but for God;
and if I do not make use of your gifts, you will find no
difficulty in placing them elsewhere. And, indeed, if I
thought you were working for me, I should be in

---

*Two of Theophane Vénard's fellow-students were yet at Paris when
the writer first visited the Seminary. One of them, Fr. Delpech,
(v. p. 96) was superior. Fr. Delpech recalled the gaiety of Theophane while at the Mission House, a disposition so pronounced,
that the future martyr was always the life of any little circle of
students among whom he might be found. [Ed.

great distress to know how to repay you for your
kindness and zeal. But, thank God, I know that it is
for Him you labor—to Him that you have devoted
your life. He reserves for you a glorious crown, and
the brightest flower in that crown will be your co-
operation in this work of the foreign missions. Oh,
what a joy would it be to me at that great day, when
the prizes will be distributed by the hand of unerring
Justice, if I might hear your name and your merit recognized and rewarded, and be permitted to sing
'Amen' to the solemn declaration which will admit
you into the land of everlasting light and love—into
the presence of our dear Lord and Saviour Jesus
Christ, and of His holy Mother, and of all His holy
angels and saints!"

Theophane was to be ordained deacon at Christmas
in 1851, and wrote with delight of the retreat which
was to precede his ordination:—

"On Sunday evening next we go into retreat till the
Saturday following, a holy and happy time of meditation and prayer, when we dwell under the shadow of
the altar, free from cares and distractions, absorbed in
God. Fancy a delicious day in spring, with a pure
sky, all nature bursting forth into leaf and blossom,
or the deep calm of a tomb. . . . Ah, it is better than
all this, for it is Heaven begun on earth, God com-
municating Himself to man, man raising and uniting
himself to God! Ah, dear friend, what happiness He
allows to His creatures!"

Then came the ordination. He writes, "The ordination was very large, and all the different communities
of Paris contributed some members. I found, kneeling side by side with me, Lazarists, Dominicans, Fran-

ciscans, Missionaries of the Holy Ghost, Irish, Negroes, etc. I knew none of them; but my heart went
out to them with love and sympathy, for are we not
children of the same Father, servants of the same
Master, soldiers of the same King? The same object
unites us; the same grace, in different degrees, was
distributed to us; the same God gave Himself to us;
and we invoked the same Queen, Mary, Mother
of the Saviour of the world. And then, as brothers,
we gave one another the kiss of peace. Oh, how
happy I was!"

Theophane had a special devotion to church music,
especially to the old hymns and canticles. He wrote
of them as follows:—

"The hymns of the Church have always had a
peculiar charm for me, and the more I hear them
the more I long to hear, and the oftener I sing them
the oftener I like to sing, for they are the voice of
man in his exile, and the voice of the Church, praying,
hoping, loving. Would that my countrymen would go
back to the good old days of a purer and stronger
faith, and not be ashamed to sing together the songs
of their forefathers! Now they care only for political
or revolutionary ditties; a malediction on those who
have swept away the faith and the hope of our people,
who have robbed them of their peace and their tranquillity! France used to be so calm and happy. But,
no; we will curse no one. Only, may God have
mercy on us all!"

But Theophane was not to see only the inside of the
Seminary. He was sent on several occasions into
the great world of Paris, and of this wonderful capital he writes thus to his brother Henry:—

"At Paris we are in the midst of the extremes of vice and virtue—vice of the lowest and most degrading kind, and virtue the most heroic! In returning from Meudon, which is our little country house, about two leagues from Paris, I constantly pass through the Bois de Boulogne. It is a magnificent park, splendidly laid out with walks and drives, shaded by fine trees, and full of beautiful flowers. It is crowded with people on foot, in carriages, and on horseback. On leaving the park you pass through the Barrière de l'Étoile, and its triumphal arch, to an avenue which leads to the Place de la Concorde. This avenue is planted with trees, and on either side you see fine houses and beautiful villas. There is even a larger crowd here than in the Bois. The greater portion are pleasure-hunters. Do they find it? Well, perhaps those do who care for nothing but dissipation and jollity. But happiness? No; happiness is to be foun' only in home and in the domestic circle where God loved and honored, and everyone loves, and hel᷍ ᷍, and cares for the other. The great cry now is, 'the People.' The word written up everywhere is 'Fraternité'—'Brotherhood.' In Paris they have well-nigh abolished the idea of family life. If I were not afraid of vexing some really good souls among them, I should say that Paris was nothing but a scene of confusion, a heterogeneous mass, where no one knew or cared for or respected the other. To realize the true meaning of Brotherhood, it should be written not on the walls, but in the heart. There is a beautiful reciprocity of feeling in the different relations of life where all are united in the one great love of Him who gave His life for us, our Lord and Saviour Jesus Christ! If only everyone could feel this, how perfect would be the harmony of earth!" . . .

To Eusebius he writes,—"You want me to describe Paris to you? Well, let us get out at the Orleans Railway Station, where the rail ends from Poitiers, and we shall find ourselves on the Quays which line the Seine, or rather which restrict it within very narrow bounds, and into which all the drains are emptied, so that the water is anything but sweet and clear like our Thouet. . . . The Tuileries garden would be the next object of interest to you, and I should praise it, like the Luxembourg, if it were not so peopled with pagan deities! Now, you are in the very heart of the Parisian world. You see splendid mansions, brilliant equipages, elegant dandies, beautiful ladies, who strut like peacocks, but who, it seems to me, need to go to school again to learn modesty, humility, and even common sense. Everybody lounges about, here, or in the museums, or in the galleries of the Palais Royal, or in the Jardin des Plantes, or in the Bois de Boulogne, where the only object seems to be to see and be seen. Here is a whole tribe of nurses with their babies; and the monkeys are showing off their tricks, and the fountains are playing, and the jugglers are trying to make people laugh. . . . Well, have not these people really earned their dinners? Then comes the evening, when everyone seems to think it necessary to go to some theatre or other, or to some ball, winding up with ice and coffee in the Boulevards, if not in a drawing-room; and the gas lights up the city all night, and the world goes to bed when the sun is rising. What a day for a reasonable being, let alone a Christian! This is Paris life, the life of people in the world who fancy they have found happiness. Frankly, the whole thing disgusts and wearies me to death. I should never end if I were to tell you how ridiculous poor human nature appears in a thousand

ways when left to itself, regardless of God, our good
God, the only end and aim of life! One gives himself the airs of a philosopher, another, of a poet; this
one has a passion for music, that one for pictures.
All talk politics, of which three parts know nothing
whatever. It is really humiliating to hear them! Oh,
you cannot think, after I have been elbowed half a day
by all these worldly people, what a relief it is to me to
come back to the Mission House! How I love its cool,
calm, quiet cloisters, the peace in its cells, the hours
of study and meditation, the gaiety of its recreations,
the charity and good will of its inmates, the charm
of its chapel, the recollection of its history, the indescribable 'something' which seems to speak to us
all day of the Apostolate and martyrdom! . . . One
day I went to Versailles; I saw its enormous castle,
and gardens, and park, but I could not feel enthusiastic
about any of them. I kept thinking, 'Well, this is
all that man can produce of magnificence and splendor.
How miserably unsatisfactory!' Ah, but all earthly
things fade so before the thoughts of Heaven! . . .
You ask me about the sights, the inventions, and the
balloons. Well, as to the last, the ladies themselves
are the most marvellous specimens! Even in heathen
times, I verily believe such things would have been
scouted. If man would give the glory of his inventions to God, they might bring a blessing; but we see
nothing, hear of nothing, but materialism and 'nature.'
God help France and Europe! . . . If you ever come
here you will be as struck as I am at the marvellous
dissipation of this place, the ceaseless turmoil, and
bustle, and noise, and unrest. Oh, how I hate these
never-ending streets, which tire my feet, my eyes, and
my ears, where the world and its views reign supreme,
and the one object of every living being seems to be

THE RIVER THOUET, ST. LOUP.

pleasure, and pleasure only! In the midst of this
impious city real saints are found, but most of those
who have eyes do not see them or know them. They
are hidden from the crowd and known only to God,
and, thank Him, they are multiplying. Oh, Christianity is not dead, as the gentlemen of the Voltaire
school are pleased to say!" . . . After dwelling a
little longer on Paris and its sights, he exclaims, "But
what is the use of my going on talking to you of all
these vanities and follies? I went the other day to
Notre Dame to see the splendid decorations which
were used on New Year's Day, 1852, when Louis
Napoleon made his triumphal entry into the cathedral. Well, what struck me most of all was the
thought of how the great ones of earth were thus
compelled to do homage to the majesty of God and
to the glory of His Church. God alone is the sovereign beauty and His works alone are perfect. If
man be ever so great, it is only when he draws his
inspirations from God, and when, in heartfelt humility, he gives to Him the glory. In Catholic countries
all human potentates seek the support of the Church,
for she is the one power—first and indestructible—
and without her aid no Catholic government can
exist, for the winds and the tempests would blow and
sweep it away from the face of the earth."

This, surely, is a noble view to take of the political
situation of a great Catholic country. In 1848 Theophane had been painfully moved by the debate in the
National Assembly; and when he came to Paris he
asked and obtained permission to go to the Chambers
and hear the principal speakers. He gave an account
of his impressions to his father, and his sinister pre-
visions were soon realized. The political horizon became more and more darkened, and the agitation was

at its height, when the *Coup d' État* of the 2nd of December gave the signal for a fresh revolution. On this event Theophane wrote as follows:—"My dearest Father,—It is ten o'clock in the morning. Paris is declared in a state of siege. The National Assembly is dissolved.". . . . Then he goes on to relate facts well known, and subjoins, "May our good God come to our aid, and direct all to His honor and glory! Let us pray for France and for all Europe. We have been expecting this shock from day to day and so we are not troubled. When and how will it all end? Human events succeed one another so rapidly and then pass away. God alone is immutable—let us go to Him! After all, what does the future matter to us? If the world were destroyed we should be safe in the bosom of His Church. The works of men alone remain—let them, then, be works of charity and justice. All this seems to me to detach one more and more from things of earth and to fix one's thoughts and heart on Heaven." To a college friend he writes, "To remedy the evil, France must be converted or else God will permit the working classes, the men who possess nothing, to be sooner or later the instruments of His vengeance. It seems to me our business is to try to become, each one of us, better, and then God will have pity upon our country. . . As far as I am concerned, I assure you I am in perfect safety. Our congregation is looked upon with a favorable eye in Paris, and everyone knows us and is kind to us. In February, 1848, on the eve of the dethronement of Louis Philippe, our community was going across the Champs Élysées. An immense crowd had collected and some deliberated what they should do to the students. But the majority exclaimed, 'Let us leave them alone.

Those are the men who are going to *martyrize* themselves in China!' and the observation saved our poor
missioners.

"The 4th of December we remained almost the
whole day near the Bois de Boulogne. A detachment
of cuirassiers had galloped toward Paris where the
fighting had begun. The workmen were in the streets,
quiet and orderly, but anxious. They were very civil
to us. The next day three of our students were obliged
to go through the streets where they had already
erected barricades. The soldiers were bivouacking
by their fires; a dense mob thronged around them, sul-
len and silent, and breathing nothing but vengeance;
but they allowed our missioners to pass without mo-
lestation, and even showed them marks of kindness
and good will."*

After the *Coup d' État,* the agitation ceased, and
people gradually became calmer. Theophane wrote
hopefully to his godmother: "The new government
seems well disposed towards religion and willing to
give the Church her due. If it goes on so, God will
send His blessing on this poor, distracted country and
there may be some chance of seeing things reorgan-
ized. Since our Lord Jesus Christ became man, His
Divine manhood must take the lead in human affairs;
for a people calling itself Christian, and throwing off
all allegiance to the Most High, becomes thoroughly
ungovernable, for the simple reason that corruption
is greater when it shows itself in what was originally
good. Those who think they can see farther than

---

*The students of the Paris Mission House are distinguishable by their
cassocks and their beards. The cassock is shorter than the average,
so as to facilitate rapid walking, long excursions being taken regularly into the suburbs. Those who are soon to depart grow beards
during the last few months, as, according to the custom of Catholic
missioners, the beard is quite universally worn in far-away countries.

their neighbors are hopeful as to the future of France, which makes me sanguine too. Although I may soon be far away, I shall always look anxiously for tidings of my country's welfare. May God bring about a brighter day! Amen." He ends with the beautiful words,—

"O my Lord, Thy people know and love Thee by instinct; but they are deceived by their chiefs, who betray and mislead them. Oh, if only all the world were of one heart and one mind to serve and honor and glorify Thee!"

CHAPTER VI.

Last Days in Paris—The Departure.

We are tempted to give one or two more extracts from Theophane Vénard's letters to his family during the remainder of his stay at the Paris Foreign Mission House; for these letters are so full of counsel, especially those to his younger brother, that we have felt they might be of equal value to others in a like position.

Eusebius had just entered the Preparatory Seminary at Montmorillon; he was fifteen, and had a strong desire to become a priest. Under these circumstances he writes to Theophane for advice; and the elder brother answers as follows:—

"My dear Eusebius,—You are now of an age to choose your future career, an age when people begin to think, and when certain convictions form themselves in their minds and influence their conduct. In your intercourse with men, you will encounter much prejudice, many strange ideas, and perversions of the truth; for their minds have wandered from the good old paths; and society in Europe has become thoroughly corrupt. I do not mean to say that there were not plenty of bad people in old times, as there are now, for man is ever the same. But formerly there were certain social bases and landmarks which none but the very vicious overstepped. For religion was the foundation of society and God gives life to nations as well as to individuals. Now all these safeguards are removed or ignored, but you will understand this better by and by.

"Well, you are asking yourself what is to be your future? Pray, simply, humbly, and fervently, to know God's will, and your path will be made clear. Then you will follow the inspiration which Divine mercy has put into your heart. Sometimes a person says, 'I will be a priest,' or 'a soldier,' or 'a landed proprietor,' and then he adds, 'Oh, such and such studies are not necessary for this or that profession!' This is the reasoning of pure idlers. Then others go on about piety: 'Piety! it is only good for priests and nuns. God does not expect so much of us!' (*How do you know?*) These are the arguments of cold and calculating natures. Now what I want you to say to yourself is, 'I am, first of all, a man, a reasonable being, created to know, love, serve, and glorify God. I come from God. I go to God. I belong to God. My body is His. My mind is His. My heart is His. I shall be judged according to my works and to the way I have corresponded to the grace given me. Well, then, God helping me, I will use this body, this mind, and this heart, as much as I possibly can for His greater glory, honor, and love.'

"My dear Eusebius, life well employed consists in this—*a faithful correspondence to grace, and a good use of the talents given*. There is no other religion than this, and the rule of life is the same for all.

"'But,' you ask, 'what does God ask of *me?*' Humility, prayer, obedience to His Divine commands and to the voice of our mother the Church, and an entire abandonment of ourselves to His Divine Providence. You answer,—

" 'But many men do not reason like this.'

"To God alone it pertaineth to judge of others. We have only to look to ourselves. For the moment, what you have to do is—study with all your might to make use of the advantages which God has put in your way, and which you owe, under Him, to the generous love of our dear father. Work not to gain honor and distinction but to please God. He who does not work for God, works for the devil and for his friend, the world. God is represented on earth by His Holy, Catholic, Roman, and Apostolic Church. She is the City of God, whose citizens we are, no matter in what corner of the earth our lot may be cast. Our Lord Jesus Christ is the chief of this city; but we shall not see this clearly until the consummation of all things. The Pope and the Bishops are His representatives on earth, and have a permanent and infallible authority to which we must submit, and in which we must believe, as in Jesus Christ Himself. He who is not with them is against them. The Catholic Church on earth is termed *Militant*—that is, she is perpetually at war with Satan and the world. Ever since her birth she has been attacked on every side. Your business must be to fight for her, and under her banner, taking the saints as your protectors and guides. . . . Do not let yourself give way to vexation at little troubles and cares. Banish the idea that such and such things *bore* you. We have to learn very early to live amidst constant contradictions and mortifications of our natural tastes and inclinations. But it is this which trains us and makes us good soldiers of the Cross, and the soul is thereby raised and purified. It is a trite saying that there is no heaven without a cloud and that you mustn't expect anything to be perfect in this life, but what I want you to do is to bear everything cheerfully and gaily, to rejoice even in vexations; and if you

can't be bright naturally, strive to be bright in and
for God. . . . Be agreeable in conversation, good-
humored and merry, full of cheerfulness and fun, and
not brooding on disagreeables. And now you will say
I have preached enough, and so I will only add, having laid down certain great principles for your life,
forward! Don't be afraid of being laughed at. You
will crown all by keeping up the tender love of a little
child for the Blessed Virgin and a confiding trust in
your Guardian Angel."

A little later he writes to him on his vocation—"You
tell me that your wishes, your tastes, a secret inspiration of grace, draw you strongly towards the priesthood. May God's Holy Name be praised! But if our
Lord calls you, you must answer. One day little
Samuel heard a voice crying out, 'Samuel! Samuel!'
'Here I am, Lord,' he replied. *Ecce ego, Domine,
quia vocasti me.* Eusebius! you think our Lord has
called you. Well, then, you must answer like Samuel,
'Here I am, Lord, what wilt Thou have me to do?
With the help of Thy grace I will do all that Thou dost
appoint, and that grace I feel will not be wanting.'

"It is, then, on the 1st of October—the month
dedicated to the angels—that you are to leave your
country and your home and your beautiful valley, to
go into a strange place. Courage! When one leaves
anything for God He rewards us a hundredfold; He
has said so Himself. But (you say) you are 'alone,'
'quite alone.' Oh, no, you are the child of our Divine
Lord and His Blessed Mother, the child of His Love,
the sheep of His pasture; have confidence in God.
Nevertheless, if there are times when your heart sinks
within you, my dearest brother, go to the chapel, offer
to our dear Lord your tears and your sacrifice, and
then, alone before God, consecrate yourself anew
without reserve to His service. Offer Him, to be-

gin with, the trials of your college life; throw yourself like a boy into the arms of Mary, and believe me
when I say you will never be forsaken.

"You will have to choose a confessor, and for this
you must pray earnestly to our Lord and His Mother
to enlighten and guide you. Then, when you have
chosen one, you must open your whole heart to him,
not only in the confessional, but when you see him
alone elsewhere; make him your friend and counsellor
in all your little difficulties and sorrows, and tell him
of your temptations and faults with thorough simplicity and openness. Then be guided by his advice,
and follow it to the letter. This is the kind of spiritual
direction necessary to one who seeks to advance
towards perfection. Confide in him entirely, and be
sure that he will keep all your little secrets as if they
were told in the confessional. You are no longer a
child, dear Eusebius, and you must begin to walk as
one worthy of the mercies of God, and of His great
designs in your behalf. Make a little book in which
you can write your impressions and your religious
feelings, now and then, putting down the date; you can
dedicate it to our Lady. Some time later you will read
them over again with pleasure, and they will serve
to brace you up when days of heaviness and weariness
overcome your courage."

(Theophane himself had this practice, but, unfortunately, when he was ill, he insisted on burning all
that he had written.)

"I should like to think that you deprived yourself
now and then of some indulgence to give to the poor.
You ought not to run into great expenses or attempt to
imitate the luxurious habits of many of those around
you. Remember your own simple home, and still more
remember how many thousands there are who suffer

5

for want of the very necessaries of life. Above all, never forget that God is in everything, in little things as in great. He ought to be the one motive of your thoughts, words, and actions. Go often to confession, have great devotion to the Blessed Sacrament, and associate yourself as soon as you can with some congregation of our Lady. Oh, how happy I was when I first became a child of Mary! Go, then, dearest brother, and may the Angel of God guide your steps! A great future is before you! a grand vocation! Think of it well, anchored on the infinite mercy of God. . . . Perhaps you will hear a voice saying, 'Come with me,' and perhaps we shall find ourselves soldiers of the same regiment, travellers on the same road, bound for the same haven. May His Holy Will be done, and not ours. Strive to fulfil with diligence and joy the work of each day ; be gay, *very* gay. The life of a true Christian should be a perpetual jubilee, a prelude to the festivals of eternity. . . . . . "

These letters abundantly show the anxious care and thought which Theophane bestowed on his brothers, who were the continual subject of his prayers, and when he became a priest, of his Masses likewise. On one occasion he wrote and told Eusebius that he was going to say Mass for him on the 1st of August, the Feast of St. Eusebius, when, from some unknown reason, he changed it to the *second* of the month. Now it happened on that very day that a thunderbolt struck the College of Montmorillon, and an electric spark fell on Eusebius, who was left for dead, and with great difficulty recovered. Eusebius always attributed this escape to the intervention of his brother, who at that very moment was offering up for him the Holy Sacrifice.

To his elder brother, Henry, Theophane writes in a
different strain; but his letters are full of suggestive
thoughts and beautifully expressed. On one occasion
he writes,—

"I am not astonished that my loving old brother
found poetry in my letters but I think that his own
heart supplied it. Talking of poetry, do you not think
that men have profaned it more than ever in these
latter days? Poetry presupposes a soul lifted above
the things of sense; it means the outpouring of a heart
full of love for God and for our neighbor, keenly
alive to the beauties of nature and of grace. The mysteries of Christianity and of the Blessed Eucharist are
eminently fitted for a poet. So also are pure love, devotion, heroism, self-sacrifice, and the rest. But when
I see men calling themselves poets, and abusing their
gift by impure allusions, and sophistries, and vague
aspirations after dreams which have no existence except in their morbid imaginations, I confess I have no
patience with them. Poetry is not meant to be merely
the exaltation and feeding of human passion by sensual indulgence. Yet three parts of the world call this
poetry. Oh, let us draw our inspirations from purer
sources! The literature of the day seems to me to run
forever either in impure or rationalistic channels, so
much so, that I dread lest we shall be all submerged
in the foul tide! I try to think of the exile going
back to his country. *He sees and thinks of nothing
else.* We are all exiles here below. Let us hasten on
to our home in Heaven. . . . I am very much struck
with the young men I have met here outside of the
Seminary. They are such contradictory creatures.
There is in them a great deal of pride with considerable
generosity; a strong love of independence with a
certain submission; much impurity with a vestige

of better thoughts learned at a mother's knee; some
courage and audacity, and yet more weakness and
foolish yielding; an ardor for work by fits and starts,
but usually inconceivable idleness; a desultory way of
living and acting without aim or purpose; in fact, the
old strife between the spirit of evil and the spirit of
good. Still among these young men there are exceptions. I know some who are living in the world, in
the very heart of great riches and luxury, and yet
are humble, pious, devout, charitable, and reverent,—
seeking out the poor in their garrets, religious 'as a
woman,' as the saying is. Their manners are simple
and natural, for they are thoroughly in earnest. They
are bright, amiable, and courteous, with faces which
prepossess one at first sight. Their lives are spent in
doing good. I don't mean to say that they don't
commit faults sometimes, for human nature is weak;
but their very failings increase their humility and
make them lean more completely on the Divine mercy.
God be praised! Such men are not very rare, though
they do not show themselves much in the streets.
There is another species, whom one sees all day long
lounging at cafés or in ball-rooms, never by themselves. They are restless, walking in a wild sort of
way, judging and criticizing everybody and everything. They neither respect nor esteem women.
They want to know everything, hear everything, and
see everything. They talk for the sake of talking,
and their least sin is that of doing nothing. . . . Such
young men swarm in the streets of Paris and their
secret lives are more pitiable than their public ones.
All young men, more or less, may rank in one or
the other of these two classes. It does not cost more
to side with the right, but then one must have a

heart and reason calmly as to the object of life,—
in a word, serve and love God.

"Good-bye, my dearest brother. Write to me soon
again. Your letters do me so much good."

But it was to Mélanie that Theophane spoke all his
most intimate thoughts and aspirations, poor Mélanie,
who had never recovered from her brother's departure,
and at last had become seriously ill. After a time she
rallied, and then her brother (whom she called her
"other half") wrote to her as follows:—

"MY DEAREST SISTER,—I am glad you have been ill,
and I am very thankful you have recovered. To explain my first proposition, which will appear very extraordinary, I feel that you have had the opportunity
to suffer something for the love of our Lord. Oh, I
am quite sure you felt the advantages of your position!
Sufferings are the money with which one buys
Heaven; therefore, your fortune is already begun.
As for me, I have not a penny. I am as poor as a
church mouse. But I hope soon to go to California.
Now do you understand my meaning? At any rate,
you know how I love you."

Mélanie had long wished to devote herself to God
in a religious life, but her brother's plans had
thwarted the accomplishment of her own wishes for a
time. She had made the sacrifice generously. Nevertheless, she felt herself strongly urged in the same
direction.

"Be comforted, my dearest sister," writes Theophane. "We are made to live together; then let us do
so in Heaven. Be patient until God opens the way for
you to give yourself entirely to Him. Perfection does

not lie in one state of life more than in another, but
consists in an entire correspondence with grace in
the position in which God has placed us. Above all,
do not be discouraged, or give way to sadness and
despondency. Your holy and hidden life in the bosom
of your family is quite as meritorious in the sight of
God, and perhaps safer than a more heroic one."

But although Mélanie was compelled to wait for a
few years to attain the great object of her wishes, she
found she could realize a portion of them by conse-
crating her virginity to our Lord, even while still
living in the world; and on this she writes to consult
her brother. He replies,—

"Your letter has filled me with great joy, for I see
how anxious you are to advance in the paths of perfection. I have joined my poor prayers with yours and
laid them at the feet of our Lady of Victories. Do
nothing hastily. You say you wish to obey your director, and you are quite right, for obedience alone is a
sure guide. You are very good to consult me, my dear
little sister; and I, who am so far below you in
everything,—I thank you with all my heart for this
fresh proof of your love. Well! what answer am I to
give you? You would not like me to say 'No,' and I
should like it still less. How can I advise you to remain in a world which I detest as you do, and which I
have left myself? I know well that for a long time
you have entirely detached yourself from its pleasures
and its frivolities; but the last act, the act of entire
renunciation, you have not yet signed and that is all
that is left for you to do. What is there, then, to stop
you? Consult your courage, consult the voice of
grace, consult those with whom you live, and if no
obstacle presents itself, may your holy desires be fulfilled. May God's will be done. Celebrate your nup-

tials, give Him your heart and your life, clothe yourself with the bridal robe, place His ring on your finger, take a new name, enter into a new family. I wish
you joy, sister *Mary,* virgin spouse of Jesus Christ!
May the day come when I shall see my much-loved
sister in the choir of virgins, of which Mary Immaculate is the Queen, and when you shall count your
brother in the ranks of apostles, and perhaps martyrs
—who knows? How joyfully we shall each then sing,
'*Regina Apostolorum, Regina Virginum, ora pro
nobis.*'† . . .

"You wish me to guess the new name you have
taken. I have puzzled my brains in vain and can find
only my own. Perhaps, in the eccentricity of your
love, you have chosen that one? And now you say
you want to be a missionary nun—a tertiary, I suppose? I have a little bit of a doubt as to the reality of
this vocation; it seems to me to taste a little too much
of fraternal affection."

But the great day came for Mélanie, and on the 15th
of July, 1852, her brother wrote again,—

"I received your cake on the Feast of St. John, you
naughty, little, spoiling sister, and I thought it very
good, though a little salt, which is the fault of your
confections. Well, be the salt of the earth! So many
souls get insipid and lukewarm. Ah, you did not expect me to preach morality to you on a cake! . . . It
is just like you and your love to remember all the little
details of that last day, and how I carried my surplice
on my arm. Ah, I am sometimes afraid you care for
me too much! Perhaps it is to punish us both that
God told me to leave you. I congratulate you with all
my heart on the step you have taken, and that you

---

†Queen of Apostles, Queen of Virgins, pray for us.

should thus have separated yourself from the world, though still living in it. God has inspired you and given you a great grace. I know you will receive it with gratitude and humility; but do not forget that your first duty is still to your family and for your family. . . . God bless you, sister *Mary Theophane*. All joy be with you in the hearts of Jesus and Mary.— Your devoted brother,   T. V."

The hour drew near when Theophane was to become a priest, and his zeal and fervor were redoubled. The atmosphere around him strengthened all these pious desires, and everything tended to help him onward in the path of perfection. In one of the corners of the garden at the Paris Foreign Mission House is a little oratory dedicated to Our Lady, and filled with candles and flowers. Every Saturday evening, and on all the vigils of her feasts, it is lighted, and the students go there to recite Litanies and sing hymns in her honor, after which follow the usual prayers at nine o'clock. But on leaving the chapel, and before retiring to his cell, each of the future missioners goes to pay a little visit to the Hall of Martyrs, a large room in which are ranged along the wall not only relics of the confessors, but the instruments of their torture and pictures of their martyrdom. Everyone stays a few minutes here to pray in silence, and then to kiss the crucifix stained with the blood of Bishop Borié. Theophane used to spend every spare moment in this room, and when the news came of the martyrdom of Father Schoeffler at Tong-king, he wrote to his sister, "Oh, if I might some day give my life like him for the Faith! I am not afraid of saying so to you, because I know your generosity and that you would not even wish to rob me of my crown. This Tong-king Mission is now the most enviable, for it is almost certain martyrdom. . . . Whatever happens, I know I may reckon on your prayers."

Every day he was getting more detached. Writing to the Bishop of Poitiers, he says,—

"Formerly, my Lord, I rejoiced in the thought of receiving at your hands the last great grace which God has deigned to bestow on me. But Divine Providence has ordered otherwise and disposed of my future. In the midst of my regrets I cannot help looking forward with joy. Yes, I own that every day I get more detached from France, even when France means to me Poitiers, and my tastes have become decidedly Chinese. I do not know what secret impulse makes me sympathize so warmly with people of another clime, be they Indians or Chinese. Some of my friends here declare I am growing like them, that I have a Chinese head, and Chinese eyes, and Chinese ways, in fact, that I am getting Chinese altogether. Do not think, however, that I have set my heart upon China. I have no other choice than the will of my superiors, that is, if they think me worthy of any mission at all, as I sometimes fear they will not. I shall always find myself too happy in the place where the Great Master will allow me to work for the welfare of my brethren and the Glory of His holy name."

Nevertheless, his superiors had no difficulty in recognizing the eminent merits of the young aspirant after foreign missions, in spite of the humility which induced him to throw a veil over all his actions; and so they hastened the time of his ordination (he was only twenty-two), and desired him to prepare himself for Trinity. He received the good news with a mixture of joy and fear, and writing to his Bishop exclaimed,—

"MY LORD,—Fruit which grows ripe before the proper time has no flavor; and here am I, a young and green fruit, which yet must be ripe in a month. In spite of this hot May sun, is it not too soon? . . I never dreamt of being called to the priesthood before Christmas, but God has disposed things otherwise. . . *'Introibo ad altare Dei, ad Deum qui laetificat juventutem meam.'* * Very soon, perhaps, another message will be brought to me, at the very thought of which my heart sings for joy. 'Pack your things, and start.' Yet when I look at myself, when I see the childish hands so soon to receive the holy oils; the feet, fresh from the playgrounds, which are to carry so far the gospel of truth and peace; my whole being, in fact, only just beginning to understand what life is, and yet so soon to teach men how to live, I can scarcely help laughing and yet crying. So mingled are my feelings and thoughts at this moment, that I can only hope in God, and beseech Him to give me strength, meekness, humility, prudence, knowledge, and charity. I trust in your Lordship's kindness that you will give me a place in your prayers, which will obtain for me the graces of which I stand so much in need."

A severe illness prostrated him for a time, but his courage and cheerfulness never deserted him; and in spite of his sufferings, which were very great, his gaiety and patience astonished his companions, who vied with one another as to who should wait upon him and do little things for him. He wrote gaily after his recovery, "I have a new body altogether, which, as

---

*I will go unto the Altar of God, to God who rejoiceth my youth.

I am going into a new country, will be very useful, and I hope we shall agree perfectly. It is a pity that I can't get a new spirit and a new heart, and then I should be altogether a new man. Pray that I may be thus transformed on the day of my ordination." He recovered sufficiently to be ordained on the 5th of June and said his first Mass the next day,—Trinity Sunday. He writes home on this occasion to his father, "My dearest Father,—Send me your blessing. I said my first Mass to-day. Oh, what a glorious day for me! True, I cannot yet meditate very well—my head is still weak and I can scarcely realize the awful mysteries of which I have become, as it were, a participator. But I feel a great peace, and am very happy. You will share in my joy, which is a family one. Would that you could have been with me on this day! But God ordered it otherwise. May we be strengthened in faith and hope; at least we shall be united in prayer."

The new missioner was at length a priest. His departure could not be long delayed, and the announcement was made to him only three days after his ordination. He gave notice to his relatives that his destination was not yet fixed, nor the actual day of farewell, but that they must be prepared for a speedy summons. He told them that he had been promised a month's notice, and added, "Dearest friends,—Courage and faith! God watches over us, and the Blessed Virgin is our protector."

The missions of his two friends, Fr. Dallet and Fr. Theurel, were already fixed; the latter was bound for Tong-king, the former for India. Fr. Dallet embarked in the middle of the month of August, and this was the first break in the chain which united these faithful friends.

But the summons for Theophane Vénard was not
long delayed, and a letter dated the 13th of September
announced his speedy departure to his family.

"My dearest Father, Mélanie, Henry, and
Eusebius,—Once more let us say together, 'God's holy
name be praised!' About a month ago five of my fellow-students received a notice to hold themselves in
readiness for departure. I was left behind until my
health should be fully regained. I could not help
grieving very much, but let that pass, for time presses.
One of the five, who had been compelled to return
home for family affairs, did not come back on the
day fixed. I have been, consequently, appointed to
replace him. I am therefore going to leave you at
once, my dearest ones, and to wish you good-bye until
our reunion in Heaven. I shall not remain even this
week in Paris; Friday will probably be my last day
on the soil of France, as we are to embark at Antwerp."

The 19th of September was to be the day of departure, and in the morning Theophane sent a farewell line to each member of his family.

"My dearest and much-loved Father,—To-day I
leave France. I must send you my last farewell; we
start at seven o'clock. On Monday we are to embark
from Antwerp; Tuesday morning we set sail. Dearest father, good-bye. My departure I know will be
a sorrow to you; to me also the separation is very
hard to bear. But courage! Life on earth passes so
quickly and death will reunite us so soon; for death
to a Christian is life, a life of eternal happiness in the
bosom of our God, in company with His angels and
His saints. *Au revoir*, then, dearest father; the way

is short, and the end is blessed. Good-bye, I embrace you with all my heart."

"MY MUCH-LOVED SISTER, MY OWN LITTLE MÉLANIE,—Good-bye. I feel it very much that I am not able to write you a good long letter. It is positive suffering to me, for we have so many, many things to say to each other, but I have scarcely a moment. I shall never forget you or our happy childhood together, or our family gatherings and home joys. By and by we shall all be reunited. I go with a heavy heart and eyes full of tears, but we must pray together, the one for the other, and bear the pain of parting bravely. God bless you. My paper must convey my last kiss to my darling sister."

"Good-bye, my dear, good Henry. Your last letter gave me so much pleasure. Oh, no, my heart is not made of stone; on the contrary, just now it melts like wax. But we shall meet again. I am going to talk of our Father who is in Heaven, and make Him known to our brothers who as yet know Him not, and perhaps I shall be first at the tryst. Pray for me. Prayer alone can soften bitterness and assuage sorrow. And I, do you think I can ever forget you? Good-bye. Let us have courage in this life and fight our battles bravely. I love you with all my heart."

"Good-bye, my poor little Eusebius. We are about to be separated but we shall be more and more closely united in thought and prayer. We must all walk straight heavenwards, no matter how rough the way. Happy those who get there first! My colleagues and I start under the best auspices, for only yesterday we heard of a fresh martyrdom in Tong-king and it is for

that mission we are bound. Good-bye! I kiss you
on both cheeks. Once more, good-bye!"

Then came the usual ceremony of departure. The
departing missioners entered the chapel after evening prayers and knelt on the altar steps. Behind them
knelt the directors of the Seminary with the student
body, as well as the friends and relatives who came to
see the young apostles for the last time. Theophane's
relatives were not of the number. After the prayers
a short meditation was given, and the assistants sat
down, the five missioners alone remaining on the
altar step standing, while one of the directors, lately
returned from a foreign mission, made a short but
touching address. Then the five young apostles approached the altar, and when close to the tabernacle
turned to their brethren, who, leaving their places,
went one by one, to kiss the feet of those who were so
soon to be our Lord's heralds, while the choir intoned
the anthem, *"Quam speciosi pedes evangelizantium
pacem, evangelizantium bona!"**†

A little episode followed, which was well described
at the time by an eminent Catholic writer.
"From the midst of the crowd of visitors an old
man came forward, walking with some difficulty, and
assisted by one of the directors of the Seminary. An
inexpressible emotion was felt throughout the chapel,
and the voices of the choir faltered as they watched

---

*The ceremony of departure now takes place several times each year.
During the Summer the date is generally fixed in August, and the
ceremonies are divided between the Blessed Virgin's shrine in the
garden and the chapel. As the chapel is not large and the main
body is reserved for choir purposes, only a limited number of the
laity may attend. [Ed.
†How beautiful are the feet of them that preach the gospel of peace,
of them that bring glad tidings.

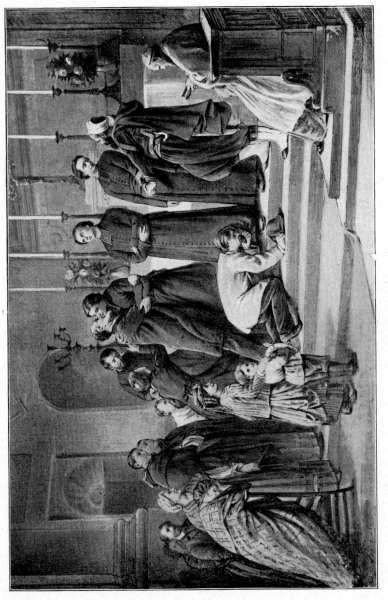

CEREMONY OF DEPARTURE.
Paris Seminary for Foreign Missions.

him slowly advancing up the aisle towards the altar.
He kissed the feet of the four first missioners, but
when he came to the fifth, the young man, as if in-
stinctively, bent forward and tried to prevent him.
But the poor old man knelt, or rather prostrated himself before him, and not only pressed his lips to his
feet, but his face and his forehead, so that his soft
white hair covered them as with a veil; and then a
sigh burst from his heart, which was more like a sob,
a sigh which was heard all over the building, and at
which everybody was moved to tears; while the poor
son himself (for it was his father) became whiter
than a sheet. Yet this was the second son which this
new Abraham had sacrificed to God, and it was the
last! . . . They assisted the old man to rise, and he
with difficulty returned to his place. The sympathy
of all present was evident, while the choir, which in
the excitement had paused for a moment, intoned the
'*Laudate pueri Dominum*'."

After this touching ceremony, the missioners themselves gave the kiss of peace to their brethren and
friends, and then followed the "*Hymn of Departure*,"
by M. Dallet. (See p. 234)

CHAPTER VII.

The Voyage—Antwerp to Hong-Kong.

OUR travellers left Paris and the Seminary with full hearts. To Theophane, especially, the parting was very bitter, for he had become attached to the Seminary, and to everything in it, in a way which only clinging, loving natures like his can understand. The young missioners managed to get together in the railway carriage, so that they might console one another; and after a time they became calm,—even joyous, so that Theophane wrote that they seemed "more like people going to a fête." Arrived at Antwerp they lost no time in going on board their ship, the Phylotaxe (lover of order), an American clipper of 600 tons, and a good, fast sailer. As a day or two elapsed before the ship was ready for sea, they spent this time seeing the quaint old Belgian town, and admiring the simplicity and devotion of its inhabitants. The embarkation took place on the 23rd of September. Theophane wrote home,—

"We bade farewell to Antwerp with a salute of nine guns, which was answered from the citadel. I am rather inclined to dreaming, and were it not for the help of God my heart would fail me altogether. You were more than half my life, and I feel the separation terribly, especially from the fact that it may be so long before I shall have any letter or tidings of you all. At any rate you are *anchored* in my remem-

brance—you see I am already getting nautical in my
expressions—and I feel as if your presence would be
ever with me, to cheer and strengthen me. We have
already passed two nights on board; how beautiful the
nights are at sea! The moon throws such a soft light
on the waves while we walk up and down the deck,
singing some national air, and smoking our cigars.
For now we are *ordered* to smoke; and a kind old
gentleman at Antwerp gave me for the passage a thousand cigars, of a mild kind, which I can manage better than the stronger ones. I sleep like a little bird in
its nest and as yet I have not been sick. The vessel
is most comfortable, the wind favorable, the crew a
picked one, the discipline admirable, and the captain
like a father. In spite of the dispensation, we abstained on Friday, as is the universal Belgian custom.
The captain never omits grace before and after meals,
and the officers are faithful likewise. I am struck
with the hard life of these sailors but I see that it
has a certain charm. I like to hear their monotonous
singing during work, and to watch them climb the
ropes; but the wonderful expanse of water, and the
thoughts which it suggests, occupy me almost exclu-
sively. I wished good-bye to every village and steeple
as we sailed past. Now we see nothing but ocean
and sky. Good-bye, then, for many months." He was
able, however, to send a few pencil lines the next
day, as follows:—

"Sunday, September 26, by a fishing-smack,
seven leagues from Calais.

MY DEAR ONES,—One more word to say that I am
well, though rather seasick. We are all bright and
cheery on board. Pray for us. Dearest Father, Mé-

6

lanie, Henry, Eusebius, once more good-bye! A last farewell to France, and to you all."

According to all human probability these were, indeed, the last words he was to send them from Europe; but a further consolation was granted to his family through a violent gale, which obliged the ship to take refuge in Plymouth harbor, where it remained three days. Theophane gave his brother an amusing account of the storm and its consequences; and adds, "This evening I have been watching a beautiful sunset on the English coast while the moon rose on the French side of the Channel. I could not help thinking about England, this country where the Sun of Truth has so long been darkened,—and praying for her with all my heart. England could do so much for the good cause, if she would only make it her own! If she only saw the truth! She reigns over the seas; but she sows error wherever her flag floats. Let us pray that this state of things may not continue. It is, I fancy, a rare sight for English people to see a priest in his cassock; for when we went into the town, men, women, and children looked at us in amazement. Some of the little ones were fairly frightened and ran away; one of the men was curious enough to come and touch one of our cassocks and examine the buttons. Then they burst out laughing, and that so naively, that we laughed too. It seems to me that they are very like the Chinese in character—curious to the verge of incivility and with little sense in their mockery."

To his sister he wrote,—

"PLYMOUTH.

DEAREST SISTER,—Peace and love and joy in our Lord Jesus Christ. Providence has willed that we should be detained here, to repair the damage done to our ship in the gale—at least, that is the reason the world gives; *I* believe it is to enable me once more to say good-bye at my ease to my friends. What do you think, dear little sister? Do you recollect how in old times, when the last of the holidays came, you and I used to take the longest road to the station, so as to prolong the time as much as possible and talk a little more? We never could agree as to which was to have the last word; we always had so much to say to each other. And now I am leaving you indeed, and probably forever! Ought we not, then, to have a good long talk? Ah, now comes the sorrow! I must have all the say to myself. There is no dear little Mélanie to answer me; no gentle eyes to look at me; no soft hand to hold in mine, and to keep it back, and try to make me stay a few minutes longer! And our good father and brother, where are they? Ah, you are all together; and I? I am alone! Alone with God —alone forevermore! But I know how you have followed me in thought; and I like to think of this letter's arrival at our home, and the welcome it will get! Am I not a real baby? But O my God, it is not wrong, is it, to love one's home, and one's father, and one's brothers, and one's sister?—to suffer terribly at being parted from them?—to feel one's loneliness? —to try to console one another?—to mingle our prayers and our tears, and also our hopes? For we have left all for Thee. We wish to work but for Thee; and we trust to be reunited one day in Thee forever and forever! You see, my darling sister, as usual, I cannot help opening my whole heart to you, who understand me so well. But let us look the thing bravely in the face. *All is over,* is it not so? An enormous distance is about to separate us. Never

again shall we meet on this earth! But after all, why
do we feel it so dreadfully? A little sooner or a
little later we shall be together again in Heaven. How
short will our separation appear to us in eternity!
Mother, friends, the SAINTS, are all gone home before
us. *Au revoir!* they said. So it is our business to
follow them and to go to them. People who are
taking a journey often go by different roads; the only
question is, which shall arrive first at the place of
destination. Well, I am going by this road, you by
that. Let the one who reaches home first encourage
the other.

"Mélanie, my sister, I leave you a precious charge
—that of our dear old father! You must help him
to pass from this world to a better. You must be his
angel of consolation and soothe his last days on earth.
Watch over our brothers, too; try to make yourself
one with them as you have been with me; and link
yourself with them in the bonds of the tenderest affection. Three are stronger than one; help one another
onwards and upwards in the rugged path of life.
Above all, let nothing separate your interests or your
affections. True love cannot be snapped asunder; it
spreads and widens, but never diminishes. Love
never dies; for it is stronger than death. God Himself has said so. The strength and increase of love
is in prayer. We are little and weak and miserable
but He who sustains us is strong and mighty. His
arms are ever stretched out towards us; let us lift
ours to meet Him.

"Life has many bitter, sad, and weary hours; often
it can scarcely be called existence. The little rivulets,
as well as the great rivers, all empty themselves into
one source—the sea. God is an ocean of love and
mercy; in Him alone is the fulness of joy. Patience

and courage, then! A little while and we shall be
with Him. He has promised it and He never belies
His word. When the little river is dried up, the
heavens give rain, and the river gaily continues its
course. When our life is arid and we are ill at ease,
let us ask for the dew and the refreshing rain and the
food from God. Our Father who is in Heaven knows
our wants, and feels for our weariness; and He sends
His ministers to supply our need. 'Ask and ye shall
receive.' Well, then, it is an understood thing, that
each of us is to help and strengthen the other, and to
make a start upwards. Short is the way and short
the time. Courage, dearest sister! my thoughts press
and tumble one upon the other; but you understand
even half a word; and you will make the others enter
into my feelings. I can speak freely only to you; but
if I write confusedly you will unravel it.

"Dear Mélanie, when you hear the priest at Mass
intone the 'Sursum corda,' think that it is I who am
speaking to you, who invite you in our dear Lord's
name to lift up your heart. Yes, mount upwards! upwards! Mount always, like a bird of passage; and
then all this sorrow will assume its just proportion,
and Heaven will be attained. Even on this sad earth,
with hearts on high, and spade in hand, we must labor
each at his task. Be patient, gentle, loving; and pray
for me, that I, working in my little furrow, may be
the same. Pray for those among whom I am going to
work, for these poor heathen brothers and sisters
of ours, for whom I would so gladly give my life.
Make your prayers thoroughly Catholic in that sense,
for such is the real meaning of the communion of
saints.

"From time to time I hope that you will write me
long letters to cheer me in my solitude, and that you

will beg our dear old friends to do the same. Think
what a joyful surprise a letter will be to me out there!
I shall send my scribblings in a Chinese guise to make
you laugh; for we must try to be gay and bright in
our correspondence and not dwell always on the
sadder side of life. And now, my darling sister, I
must come to a stop. There is a limit to everything,
even to these closely-written pages! My heart rests
on your heart and my hand in yours. Adieu. You
understand? God bless you, my dearest sister!"

From Plymouth Theophane wrote also a few lines
to his little brother:—

"Bless our Lord, and the rain and the winds and
the tempests which have blown me into this town of
Plymouth, that I might write one word more to my
dear little Eusebius! Our good-bye has been said,
and our lives will henceforth run in different channels
—unless you come to have a Chinese taste like me! I
turn my back upon you, but not my heart, you will
understand! Our thoughts will ever be united, in our
prayers as in our work. You are going back to college. Work! work! work! Time is more precious
than you realize. Learn all you possibly can, but
especially languages; for people fraternize a great
deal more than they used to do, and this fusion
should tend to the triumph of truth. Try to coöperate
in this great work. I leave you to the care of your
good angel. May he guard and protect your youth
and your whole life! Dear brother, we shall see
each other in Heaven. I give you for advice the
same words I gave Mélanie, 'Sursum corda.' May
God give you the fulness of His grace, patience,
peace, and joy, in life and death! Amen."

These letters were dated the 7th of October. Two days after, the voyagers left the port of Plymouth, and no news was received of them till the April following, when a letter arrived from Singapore, dated February. Theophane wrote a long and detailed account of the passage, but as all long voyages resemble one another, we will confine our extracts to a few personal details:

"We are entering the harbor," wrote Theophane from Singapore. "So I will prepare my home letters, and I am glad to do so on New Year's day. This morning my first thought after God was for you all. On the 10th of October, Sunday evening, we left Plymouth. Another Belgian vessel, the 'Atalanta,' left the port at the same time, with a hundred and sixty passengers who were going to the gold-fields. What a poor object! You may believe that not for all the gold in Australia or California would I have left you all! Our vessel is a very fast sailer, and our captain a model of all virtues, religious from conviction, speaking little but always to the point; he has his ship in perfect order, and is immensely popular with his men; his courtesy and kindness to us could not be exceeded. The days are long and monotonous on board ship; the sight of a few strange birds, one or two swallows, flying-fish, and porpoises, with a shark here and there, these are the only events in a long voyage. The sea, I confess, wearies me to death. It is certainly fine to see great waves rolling one over another, but I should prefer seeing it from *terra firma*. We had the unspeakable consolation of daily Mass for the first month and a half; but afterwards our altar-breads got spoiled. How I have longed for the possibility of paying a visit to the

Blessed Sacrament, or of assisting once more at some
Catholic ceremony! When the body is deprived of
food, it languishes and dies; and it is the same with
the soul, without the Bread which sustains its life. . . .
Time and again I found myself dreaming on deck,
leaning against the bulwarks, and looking back on
my past life—my happy childhood, my darling mother,
my father's sacrifices, my education, our joyous home-
gatherings, my life at school and at college. . . . And
now here I am, in the hands of Providence, full of
thankfulness for past mercies and blessings, full of
hope for the future. My dear father, in your last
letter, consenting to my departure, you encouraged
me by saying, 'The hand of God is everywhere.'
This shall henceforth be my motto. The hand of God
is everywhere; therefore it will be everywhere with
me. . . . On our arrival at Singapore we heard,
without much astonishment, of the proclamation of
the empire. God grant peace to our dear France!
In this country it seems to me that gold is the supreme
god. New mines are daily discovered; but I never
heard that men found in them peace or happiness. It
is charity alone which is pure gold, gold tried in the
furnace; the rest is but false money."

Our missioners were still at Singapore, when there
arrived several young Cochin-Chinese students who
had been sent by Bishop Gaultier to the College of
Penang. The sight of them made Theophane's heart
beat more quickly than ever, and he wrote to Father
Dallet,—

"Every evening these young men pray together in
their own language, and we put our ears to the cracks
of the door to hear them. Their singing is so sweet!
Such plaintive, touching tones! And shall I tell you
all? They are real heroes that we have next to us,

men on whose heads a price has been put for leaving
their country. They are the sons, the brothers of
martyrs, and they come from Annam, the land of
martyrdoms."

After spending three weeks at Singapore, Father
Vénard and two of his companions started for Hong-
Kong. The rest remained a few days longer, till
a favorable opportunity presented itself for going to
their respective destinations. Before leaving Singapore, Theophane wrote a few lines to the great friend
and companion of his boyhood, a young lady living
near his old home:—

"I like to think that you remember our old walks on
the hillside, and the pleasant readings we used to have
together. I assure you I have a faithful memory and
I never can think of those happy days without emotion. All my friends have a place in my heart and
the thought of them often brings tears to my eyes,—
not that I regret what I have done, for it seems to me
that I simply followed the inspiration of God's grace,
but because this separation from those so dear to me
cannot take place without a terrible wrench, and when
the wound is reopened it bleeds.

"You tell me that you are full of troubles and
trials. I can well believe it; and I ask of God to give
you strength and grace to bear them. You know
how deeply interested I am in everything that concerns
you. Ah, one must own that life on this earth is a
poor thing at best; there is scarcely a day without a
cloud! Sorrow and suffering are found everywhere;
they are the daily bread of each of us. The thing is
to know how to use them. Happy those who know
how to turn them to advantage! Such souls will be

amply recompensed hereafter. I always look upon these miseries as a kind of money with which to buy Heaven; but then this money must bear the image of Jesus Christ, just as our ordinary coinage bears the superscription of the king or queen of the country where it is struck. Courage, then, courage! Our King loves you and calls you to Himself by His own way, the royal road of the Cross. Try to love it for His sake, and to follow Him gladly, when and where He calls you. When we shall meet each other again in the place where we all hope to be reunited, you will be rich in glory, for you have been rich in sorrows and in merits!"

CHAPTER VIII.

In Hong-Kong—Final Preparation.

From Singapore our missioner proceeded to Hong-Kong, where he arrived after a long and tedious passage on board an English sailing-ship. The joy he experienced on landing made him exclaim, "I feel all the more keenly how great a rest it will be to quit this stormy sea of the world, and to repose in our good God!" He was a little disappointed not to find at Hong-Kong the letters which were to fix his future destination; but he consoled himself with the thought that he was not yet fit for the heavy charge of the apostolate. A still greater disappointment arose from finding no letters from home—not even one from his sister! He felt this keenly and his loneliness pressed upon him heavily for the first few weeks. When tidings from his family at length arrived, he broke into a song of joy to his father, as follows:—

"Oh, your letters did me so much good! I love them as one loves the dew after great heats, as the traveller in the desert rejoices at the green oasis where he and his camels can rest and find shade and water. For we poor missioners live, as it were, in a desert, and that always. When we get news of our loved ones at home, of our country, of our friends, how happy it makes us! I feel a thousand times stronger when I have read and re-read your dear letters, for your sympathy fortifies and encourages

me. I no longer feel alone in my sacrifice; others
share in it and live, as it were, with me in thought and
heart. God be praised for the home-love in which I
have been cradled and for the dear friends He has
given me! I am as a branch of a tree, and no longer
dried up by being separated from the parent stem,
for the same loving sap runs through us all. God is
surely very good to our human hearts, which He has
formed, and of which He knows the yearnings and
the weaknesses; and then He is the same in China
as in France, and what do we want beside Him on
earth or in Heaven!"

Fr. Vénard stayed fifteen months at Hong-Kong.
During this time he devoted himself to learning the
Chinese language, in itself a most arduous and weari-
some task, for the different dialects are innumerable,
and though he put his whole heart into it, yet his
health, which was affected by the great heat, often
prevented his studying. When this was the case he
used to take long walks by the seashore or in the
mountains, trying to become acquainted with the
people and their habits; and although their hypocrisy
and vanity often disgusted him, still the modesty of
the women, and their careful decency in dress and
manner, often contrasted favorably with the customs
of his own countrywomen. What drove him almost
to despair was the bad example given to the natives
by Europeans calling themselves Christians, who, as
he expressed it, "wherever they went, spoiled God's
work." But his special indignation was aroused by
the conduct of the English engaged in the opium
trade. He writes to his sister,—

"This opium is a substance extracted from the

poppy and is smoked like tobacco. The result is a positive destruction of all the faculties of mind and body, ending in complete stupefaction. The Chinese have a passion for this pernicious drug, and the English an equal anxiety to supply them with it; they bring it from Hindustan. In spite of treaties and protestations, the sums acquired in this contraband traffic are enormous, and the trade is a thorough disgrace to the English nation. If the devil had tried to invent something to ruin men, body and soul, he could not have hit on anything more effectual. I wish we could have an association of prayers to try to put down this infamous traffic."

Writing to Father Dallet about the Chinese insurrection, he says, "Nothing can be more terrible at this moment than the state of China. But the melancholy thing is that European agents are at the bottom of it, and vainly expect, by coquetting with the rebels, to promote a Protestant movement among the people. Never was there such a delusion! . . . The worst of it is that it all adds to the hatred of the Chinese toward strangers; so that when the Emperor succeeds in defeating the rebels, which is inevitable, his vengeance will fall on the Europeans, and especially on the missioners. . . . You ask me, 'What are the rebels about?' Nobody knows. The French and the English papers write long articles, and give their readers astounding intelligence of battles fought and won, and develop grand theories as to the future of the Chinese Empire; but they are all the dreams of editors. Every one laughs at them here, for there is not a word of truth in their statements; and as to the marvellous changes which this rebellion is to bring about, I think they will find that the mountain has brought forth a mouse! They talk, too, of the

energetic representations made by the French and the
English ministers in favor of Christianity; all this is
pure invention. The spirit of Constantine and of St.
Louis is far from being that of modern governments,
which have all become more or less atheistical under
the influence of Protestant, rationalistic, and infidel
doctrines; expediency is their watchword. As for us,
in God alone is our hope and succor. Let us pray,
then, more and more fervently for the conversion of
the infidels."

The numbers of letters which we find written by
Theophane to his old friend, Father Dallet, prove that
their affection had not been cooled by distance or
separation. We give an extract from one written on
the 26th of September, 1853:—

"You ask me, dear old friend, if you live as much
as ever in my remembrance. Oh yes, quite as much!
I love you with a special and devoted attachment, and
you must not be scandalized at it. It is surely allow-
able to have a warm, particular friendship, especially
when one is so far away from its object, and the
community will not be the sufferers. I have a full belief and confidence that God does not disapprove of it;
for it is in Him and for Him that our hearts have
been united. It is not the evil which is in us that
unites us in this tender bond of love, but our higher
and better aspirations. Let us, then, be forever *one*,
my dearest brother, united in the same work, devoted
to the same cause, humble disciples of the same
Master. . . . Our feet toil painfully here on earth,
but our thoughts soar above. . . . My bishop wrote
to me, just before I left Paris, 'I pray for you to our
dear Lord, that your devotion may daily become more

perfect, that your holocaust may be complete, and that having embarked in so great a work, you may persevere in it after the manner of the saints. *Do not be an Apostle by halves,* my dear child.' . . . Now I have these words always before me, and they give me courage and strength; and I have copied them for you that you may use them too. . . . I have been laughing at the idea of your beard, of which you fancy I shall be envious; but I assure you my moustache is quite enough for me. . . . Dearest friend, I am afraid you are very much tried in your present mission. If I were only by your side to grasp your hand and share all your troubles, as of old! I know you so well that I feel the more for your peculiar trials. But it is always the same; the gold must pass through the furnace. God will prove and try you, and having fed you with milk, He is now weaning you for stronger and greater things. Don't let us be *'Apostles by halves!'* It's a great thing to be a missioner! Our duties are without limit, and imply perfection, if possible. All the miseries you picture to me I feel and see vividly, and my heart bleeds for you. I feel that my own soul is strengthened by suffering, and that from one's very wounds arise greater vigor, firmness, and courage. You tell me of all these sad things, but you add, 'Happy are those who can keep themselves apart, and live in the still silence of their own hearts with God.' May God pour into your wounds the wine and oil which alone can heal them, and make you taste the sweetness as well as the bitterness of His cross! . . . Well, I must stop. My heart could go on forever to you, but my head and hand are tired. I repeat constantly for us both my favorite little ejaculation *'Jesu, mitis et*

humilis corde, miserere nobis!* In fact, I say these
words so constantly to myself that they have become
a habit. I hear you exclaim, 'Ah, he is going to preach
again!' No, for once you are wrong. I am not going
to give you any more bad advice but try to become
more humble and amiable myself. God bless you,
dearest friend and brother."

Theophane had many warm college friends besides
Father Dallet; and among these we must mention the
Abbé Theurel, afterwards Bishop of Acanthus. These
links were never broken till the end, for Theophane
looked upon them, "as given by God, that each soul
might be helped upwards by mutual love in the heavenly race." After some weeks spent at Hong-Kong,
Fr. Theurel left for Tong-king, leaving Theophane to
follow him later. This separation with the last of his
fellow-travellers was very trying to our missioner,
who consoled himself by writing certain stanzas in
honor of his friend. He always had a great taste
and talent for poetry, and often used to say that he
had to guard himself, like Father Faber, lest it should
absorb him too much. Other friends from the Paris
Seminary soon joined him, among whom was Father
Chapdelaine, who was much older than Theophane,
being about forty. Theophane describes Fr. Chapdelaine as "a Norman, with an iron constitution,
frank, gay, and loyal in character, a capital companion,
and above all, a holy and courageous missioner."
Writing to Fr. Dallet, he adds, "Father Chapdelaine
(who sends you his best love, by the by) is only
waiting till his little lodging is prepared, to start. He
is the healthiest, the most active, and the jolliest of
us all; and Father Bariod might well say on his

---

*Jesus, meek and humble of heart, have mercy on us.

FR. PROSPER DELPECH,
Director at the Paris Seminary for Foreign Missions.
(A former classmate of Theophane Vénard.)

birthday that he had 'the rosiness of perpetual youth.'" After a few years of arduous toil in the mission of Kwang-si, this joyous, ardent spirit received in 1856 the crown of martyrdom! But we are anticipating.

Near the town of Hong-Kong a college had been established for the Canton mission, under the patronage of St. Francis Xavier. Fr. Guillemin was the head of this college, and he asked Fr. Vénard to come and teach Philosophy to the students who had made their first studies at Penang, another missionary college. Theophane gladly accepted, delighted to find some definite work during this time of weary waiting, and especially to be under the direction of a man whom everyone looked upon as a saint. A few years later this same Fr. Guillemin came to Europe, was consecrated Bishop at Rome, and then paid a visit to France, bringing with him a young Chinese who had been Theophane's pupil. Eusebius Vénard was at that time in the Seminary and describes Bishop Guillemin's visit to Poitiers as follows:—

"It was on the 30th of January, 1857, that Bishop Guillemin came to the Seminary to talk to us about his mission. The first day I could not get a private conversation with him, but I made acquaintance with Benedict, his Chinese companion, and began talking to him about Theophane. The moment I mentioned his name, Benedict's face lit up with joy, and one could see that the name awoke in him the fondest recollections; from that moment we became like brothers. The next day I was presented to the Bishop; he looked at me attentively, and seeing in me a likeness to my brother, exclaimed, 'Oh, my dear Abbé! my good Abbé!' and was much moved. Then he

7

began to talk of Theophane, of his zeal and devotion, of his bright, gay, frank manner, of his distinguished talents, of the way he was beloved, and of his ingenious charity and kindness towards everyone. He added, 'When I was made superior of the Canton mission, all the students, with Theophane at their head, came to congratulate me, and to recite some verses which he had composed in my honor. He had even made a mitre and crozier of bamboo, with a playful allusion to their being a prophecy of what they most wished,—a dignity to which, unhappily for my poor self, I have now arrived. But this cheerful, bright disposition of his was of immense use to me in directing the college. The students idolized Father Theophane, and he kept up an admirable spirit among them, which enabled them to make light of every hardship and difficulty. He went with me one day up a high mountain, from which he could see what he called his "Promised Land." Never did I see him so joyous. Ah, your brother is indeed a perfect missioner and I have done nothing but regret his departure for Tong-king, for I loved him very much, and he belonged to me first of all!' He then gave me many little details of his daily life, too long to write, but all showing his deep affection for my brother, and his thorough appreciation of his merits."

It was in the month of February, 1854, that Father Vénard received his orders for the Western district of Tong-king. He wrote at once to express his joy to Fr. Barran, Superior of the Foreign Mission Seminary at Paris.

"Very Rev. Father Superior,—Tong-king for China, I shall not lose much by the exchange! I should have liked any mission which was awarded

me; but that of Tong-king, under the care of Bishop
Retord, so full of holy associations and blessed recollections, oh, this is indeed the post I should most
ardently have coveted! I love it as being the heritage
which the great Father has awarded to me. I love it
because it is the grandest mission of all, 'the Diamond
of Asia,' as a poet has called it. When I was at Paris,
and so unhappy at being left behind, when my brothers
had all been sent to their respective destinations, Fr.
Albrand, to console me, said, 'Do not be cast down,
this is not a case of *tarde venientibus ossa!*†—I like
to think of this, and I beg of you to express my
gratitude to that dear, good Father for all his kindness
towards me."

Theophane wrote also to his family. "Well, my
dear people, I am going to Tong-king. There the
venerable Charles Cornay died a martyr. I do not
say that the same fate is reserved for me; but if you
will only pray ardently, perhaps God may grant me a
like grace. . . . I am not going to China, which I have
seen as Moses saw the promised land; but I must
guide my boat to another shore, a shore on which Frs.
Schoeffler and Bonnard (one on the 1st of May, 1851,
the other on the 1st of May, 1852) obtained the
martyr's palm.* It is in the Annamite country, which
includes Tong-king and Cochin-China, where the spirit
of persecution is most active. A price is put on the
head of each missioner, and when one is found, they
put him to death without hesitation. But God knows
His own, and only to those whom He chooses is the
grace of martyrdom given. One is taken and the

---

†Bones to the late comers.

* Fathers Cornay, Schoeffler and Bonnard were all former students
of the Paris Mission Seminary. Frs. Schoeffler and Bonnard were
decapitated; Fr. Cornay was not only decapitated but dismembered.

other left; and there as everywhere His Holy Will is
done. In spite of the violence and the universality of
the persecution there, the missions are the most flourishing. *'Sanguis martyrum semen Christianorum.'*†
We run the risk likewise of being cut off by pirates in
the passage from Hong-Kong to Tong-king; but that
must be as God permits. . . . This mission, to which
I am appointed, is indeed a great one,—in its organization and in the number and fervor of its converts, who
amount to upwards of 150,000 souls; greater still in
its hopes; in its native clergy, who number 80 priests,
and 1200 catechists; in its religious communities, for
there are upwards of 600 Sisters; in its seminaries,
with more than 300 students; in its chief pastor, of
whom the highest praise that can be given is, that
since his episcopate, he has added 40,000 sheep to his
fold. Is not that a noble escort with which to mount
to Heaven? a beautiful crown for all eternity? I
cannot tell you with what impatience I am looking
forward to being under so holy a bishop, to be initiated
by him into the apostolic ministry, to be trained in his
school, and to march, as a simple soldier, under the
orders of so great a general. There are already six
missioners under him from the Foreign Mission
Seminary. May I make a worthy seventh! And
then think of the martyrs,—those real glories of Tong-
king, those immortal flowers gathered by our Lord's
own hand in the garden of His predilection. These
martyrs are the patrons and protectors of the mission;
their blood, shed in the great cause, is always pleading
for us before God, and the remembrance of their
triumph gives fresh courage to those who are still in
the strife. Only think what an honor and what a

---

†The blood of martyrs is the seed of Christians.

happiness it would be for your poor Theophane, if
God deigned, . . . you understand. *'Te Deum lauda-
mus* . . . . *Te martyrum candidatus laudat exer-
citus'.''†*

He wrote also to his old friend, Father Dallet; and
as if martyrdom was the great object of his life, he
exclaimed, "Only a few years ago Frs. Galy and
Berneux were seized on their arrival at Tong-king;
if the same good luck could only befall us! Oh, dear
old friend, every time the thought of martyrdom
comes across me, I thrill with joy and hope! But
then this better part is not given to all. I dare not
aspire to so brilliant a crown, but I cannot help
feeling a longing and sighing for such a grace.
*'Domine qui dixisti: majorem charitatem nemo habet
ut animam suam ponat quis pro amicis suis.'*‡ You do
not forget our mutual prayer. It has for me an
inexpressible charm: *'Sancta Maria, Regina Martyrum, ora pro nobis!'*†† Pray, pray for your poor
little friend, who never forgets you, no, not for a
single day!"

To his brother Henry he wrote, "How well I
understand what you meant when you said, 'Eusebius
has arrived fresh and well, so that we are ALMOST a
complete family party.' And I, poor little I, on the
contrary, am going farther and farther away! Ah! I
assure you my thoughts travel back to St. Loup very,
very often, and the tears come into my eyes when I
think of you all and our happy home, and all the joys
of my childhood and youth. Never since my departure
have I known family happiness and real love; such

---

†We praise Thee, O God. The white-robed army of martyrs gives
                    praise to Thee.
‡O Lord, Thou who hast said, " Greater love than this no man hath,
      that he lay down his life for his friends."
      ††Holy Mary, Queen of Martyrs, pray for us.

things are not to be met with every day! But I
expected it. I felt that it was inevitable. All I can
hope is, that after the wound will come the healing.
Every age, every position has its cares, its pains, and
its bitternesses. Nothing except what comes from
God is good here below; but we have much to thank
Him for, and especially for the grace which makes us
His friends. . . . Do not think of me as sad; on the
contrary, I am very happy and bright; when one is
working and living for God, one's heart is at ease.
And you, you say, are all day scribbling on musty
papers. Well, office life has its charms for some. For
me, had I not chosen a different path, I should have
preferred to work in the fresh air. The day's
shooting you tell me of brought back such pleasant
recollections of the good old times. I could have
fancied myself there! At Tong-king I wonder what
I shall find. Not much game, I fancy. Well, one
finds our good God everywhere, and He is our
happiness and our joy. There is no use in being
sad, so that in the midst of discouragement and
disgust, and every kind of mental suffering, one must
try to take one's heart in both hands, and force it to
cry out, 'Welcome joy all the same!' The soul finds
itself in such a different state at different times; some
days, gay and calm, and at ease; other days, sad and
weary, and broken-hearted. This is the case with
everybody who is not a phenomenon. I believe it is
the struggle between the upper and the lower parts
of our nature. When our better half triumphs, we
are at peace; but when we let ourselves go, and
yield to our natural inclinations, then comes a state of
disorder, of anxiety, of longing after the impossible,
of dissatisfaction with our lot and with the position
in which God has seen fit to place us. This state

of mind must be vigorously resisted, for it obscures our judgment and falsifies our ideas. Now there are certain things which strengthen the ascendency of evil thoughts in us, and these are bad companions, bad books, a forgetfulness of daily duties, and consequent vicious habits. But of all these, bad books are the worst. They are the plague of the present day. A book is bad not only when it contains impure and immoral thoughts, but when it gives false ideas, pretending to judge of everything, to ridicule everything sacred or venerable. Such books are all the worse when they are beautifully written, as they often are; they vitiate the taste and give a disgust for all healthy food. I knew a young man in the navy whose mind had been completely poisoned by this kind of reading; and when he came to realize the evil of it, you cannot imagine how he expressed himself to me about these pernicious books. My dearest brother, forgive me for saying all this; but I know your passion for reading, and all I venture to say is, do not play with poison."

To his favorite sister he added a few words of farewell. She had told him that having, for fun, drawn lots at Christmas as to who should represent the different personages at the Nativity, she had drawn the name of "Mary;" but Theophane's lot had fallen on that of the ass. In reply, Theophane says gaily, "I am very much pleased at the portion awarded me in your drawing. I am to be the ass. Very well. I won't accuse you of a little bit of mischief in the matter, but accept my part. The ass knows how to bray; that is to teach me to be a good trumpeter of the Gospel. The ass receives blows without complaint: may his patience be my model. Again, the poor animal is treated with scorn and derision, his very name is the reverse of a compliment; but he goes on his way just the same. Well, like him, I must disregard human opinion, cultivate humility, bear to be despised, and follow my Lord and Master everywhere, always, and in spite of all. As for you, my darling little sister, you have indeed chosen the better part. Guard it carefully. It is a life of recollection, of union with God. I fancy your sitting like Mary at Bethany, at the feet of Jesus, listening to His Word,—gentle, attentive, loving, and caring nothing for the world outside. Your life must be not only the active one of Martha, but the contemplative one of Mary, for both were united in the Mother of our dear Lord. The true science of piety, in fact, consists in reconciling these two. I know you love best to be Mary, but when duty compels you to act as Martha did, do not be *only* Martha, full of anxiety, and 'careful about much serving.' Do the works of Martha with the spirit of Mary; let the interior life leaven the exterior, conforming your will to the Will of Jesus. Dearest sister, imitate Jesus, imitate His holy Mother, and you will be indeed perfect."

CHAPTER IX.

Arrival at Tong-king.

On the 26th of May, 1854, Theophane Vénard, with an older missioner who was returning to Tong-king, said good-bye to Hong-Kong, and as the wind was favorable, a few hours' sail brought them to Macao, where they were most kindly and hospitably entertained by the Spanish Dominicans. Fr. Vénard, speaking of this town, says, "When the Portuguese were masters of the sea, Macao was an important place. Ships of all nations were anchored in its harbor, and it was the centre and emporium of all the European commerce with China. The numberless missioners who have watered the Chinese soil with their blood all started from Macao, whence they spread themselves to the remotest confines of this great empire. Portugal had a noble mission assigned to her by Providence, but she misunderstood and rejected it. This brought her downfall, and it seemed as if God had broken her as one breaks a useless or worn-out instrument. The kings of the earth have never gained anything in their strifes with the Church of Jesus Christ and against His vicar on earth, and their victory is magnificently rendered in the Psalms, 'Et nunc, reges, intelligite; erudimini qui judicatis terram.'† Macao is indeed a ruin. There is a gov-

---

† And now, ye kings, understand; learn, ye who judge the earth.

ernor, it is true; but he has no longer any *prestige*.
Soldiers still mount guard but their number is miserably small, and no one has any money to pay them.
There are fine houses, but those which are not shut
up are occupied by English or Americans. A rich
Portuguese scarcely exists; but the poor actually
swarm. The Chinese alone still maintain some kind
of trade. Hong-Kong gave the death blow to Macao.
There are a few curious things to be seen in the old
colony, among them the tomb of Camöens, buried between two rocks in the midst of the most beautiful
scenery, just such as one might imagine should be the
grave of a poet. This tomb forms the principal orna-
ment of a garden, which, unfortunately, is poorly kept.
It is a place much frequented by strangers, and some
of them have had the bad taste to cut their names in
the rock; others (among whom, I am sorry to say, are
some French sailors) have written stupid and even
indecent rhymes on the slab above."

On the 2nd of June our two missioners left Macao,
and we read the following account of their journey
in the letters of Theophane to his family:—

"TONG-KING,
The Eve of St. John, June 23, 1854.

MY DEAREST BROTHERS,—To you I am going to
write my first Tong-king letter. I arrived safe and
sound at the mission of the Spanish Dominican
Fathers, and I write now to give you some details of
our voyage. Fr. Legrand and I embarked at Macao
on the 2nd of June, towards evening. We thought
our Chinese captain would weigh anchor immediately.
Not a bit of it. A Chinaman will never do anything
directly. They had to deliberate as to the voyage,

consult the Devil, take precautions against pirates, etc.
We were to sail in company with other Chinese junks;
but the Chinese mistrust one another, and before
making an actual start, they feign to go several times,
to see if the other ships are ready and trustworthy.
There we were, two poor European missioners, among
a people who don't admire anything from Europe,
and who are always ready to insult those who do not
inspire them with fear. We were thrust into a little
hole where we could only sit or lie down, breathing
foul air, and covered with vermin. Here we had to
stay day and night, for if we attempted to leave it
the Chinese called us 'Foreign Devils,' and amused
themselves by examining all we had on, and all that
we did. If the departure was delayed, if the wind
blew, if we were threatened by pirates, it was *we* who
were to blame. It was impossible to please them. If
we tried to be kind or familiar with them, they insulted
us; if we talked little, and maintained a certain gravity
and reserve, we were cold and haughty. The only
source of strength and consolation to the missioner in
these miseries is the cross. He thus passes over many
things which would otherwise irritate and wound; so
we can maintain a certain equanimity, a necessary
virtue in the East, though sometimes rather difficult to
attain. But the courier is waiting. . . . We set sail
at last, in company with seventy vessels, whose
skippers, after parleying, had come to an understanding
with our captain; they were obliged to make a for-
midable appearance in numbers so as to intimidate
the pirates. We caught sight of six of the latter's
vessels in a place called Tin-Pac, and being well armed,
we fired upon them with the small cannon in our
bows; they retreated, and we made all sail towards
Haï-Nan, a large island, where we remained several

days, anchoring under a town which is said to contain
two hundred thousand inhabitants. We did not dare
to land, or in fact, to show ourselves in any way. One
of our missioners from the diocese of Poitiers, Fr.
Bisch, is working here, but we could only salute him
with our hearts. On leaving Haï-Nan, the Chinese
junks separated, only a small number steering for
Tong-king. Until then the sea had been calm and
beautiful; afterwards it became windy, and I paid my
usual tribute to the fishes. . . . Two days later we
sighted the shores of Tong-king. I cannot tell you
my feeling as we neared the place of disembarkation.
I offered myself again to God, begging Him to dispose
of me for His glory and honor, and I invoked my
Mother Mary, and my guardian angel, and the Patron
Saints of Tong-king. . . . The general view of the
country is magnificent,—rich plains, with grassy hills,
a luxuriant vegetation, such as one reads of in
Robinson Crusoe, and the whole backed by a superb
range of snowy mountains. We entered the harbor by
the mouth of a beautiful river which glided through
woods and gardens till we cast anchor at a place called
Cuâ Câm, which is the centre of the contraband
Chinese trade. We were no longer allowed to see
the light of day, and even at night we dared to breathe
the fresh air on deck only with very great precautions.
This state of things lasted (fortunately for us) not
more than forty-eight hours. The mandarin of the
Custom House came to inspect our vessel. We could
see this august personage through the cracks of our
prison, while we scarcely ventured to breathe and most
carefully abstained from all noise or movement; but
the old fox returned to the shore without having
scented the nest. The next day a Christian boat came
for us, for nearly all the inhabitants of Cuâ Câm are

Christians. There was a misunderstanding between
our Christians and the crew; but the Christian rowers,
seeing that we were not afraid, took courage and
managed to bring us in a few hours to the flourishing
Mission House of the Spanish Dominicans. Bishop
Hilarion Alcazar received us in his episcopal *palace*
(which, you must understand, is in these countries a
simple hut or cabin), and treated us with that generous
and delicate hospitality which makes one think of the
early Christians. He has insisted on my resting here
a few days to recover from the effects of the late
voyage, and I am enjoying that ineffable peace and
joy which seems to me especially sent by our Lord to
His missioners."

Fr. Vénard continues his recital to his sister a few
weeks later as follows:—

> "WESTERN MISSION, TONG-KING,
> *Vinh-Tri, July* 31, 1854.

MY DEAREST SISTER,—You have doubtless read my
letter to Henry and Eusebius, describing our voyage
from Macao to Tong-king; we heard afterwards
that if we had delayed our landing for a few hours
only, the news of our death would have followed that
of our arrival; for three royal ships, having heard a
rumor of our coming, surrounded the Chinese junk
in which we had taken our passage, and examined her
minutely in every part, as well as other vessels, so that
no escape would have been possible. But God preserved us, and at that very moment we were enjoying
the refined hospitality of Bishop Alcazar. We stayed
there eight days but I was ill all the time. An Annamite doctor gave me some kind of tonic which enabled
me at last to continue my journey. You will wonder

at hearing me talk of doctors and medicines, as you probably imagine that I am in a country of savages. But you must know that the civilization of the Anna-mites equals, if it does not surpass in some points, that of Europe; and they possess physicians of undeniable skill and very high reputations in the country. The one who attended me could tell at once by the pulse the nature of my malady and said that it arose from derangement of the liver. From Bishop Alcazar's we went on to Bishop Hermozilla, a vener-able man, like an ancient column standing amidst the ruins. Nothing can equal the simplicity and piety of this good old bishop. One day, while we were there, the heads of the mission came to him with a complaint that the peasants had not paid up what they call 'the rice of the Blessed Virgin,' a species of tithe for the maintenance of the altars, levied on the congregations, and put under Our Lady's protection. The bishop took the side of the poor, as the rice harvest that month had failed, and he finally gained their cause. We stayed only two days at this episcopal *palace*. Don't let the name mislead you. A bishop's residence here means a poor cabin, half wood and half mud, thatched with straw. The houses are all of the same kind and it is easy to get used to them, for the climate is very hot. All one needs is protection from the sun and the rain.

"The churches are not more beautiful. A straw roof, sustained by wooden pillars, which are hung with silk on festivals, that is all our splendor. A few rough boards form the altar. If the Annamite Church enjoyed any kind of peace, even for a time, more sumptuous temples would be built. But now it is not worth while to construct anything but temporary buildings, which may be removed at the breaking out

of any fresh persecution. After a few days we started
for the Central Vicariate of the Spanish Fathers. We
were to have gone by water, but the wind was against
us. So we had to be transported in hammocks,
according to the custom of the country, and in this
way to traverse many pagan villages. Once we passed
near a great market or fair which was being held on
the roadside. We were just in the middle of this
fair, when we came upon the house of a mandarin,
the *great man* of the place. Now it is a rule that all
travellers, unless of superior rank, shall go on foot
before these residences, to testify their respect. We
did not dare to conform to this usage and thereby
show ourselves to the crowd. Our bearers quickened
their pace to a trot. Presently came the cry after us,
'Who are those men that do not get down from their
nets?' The catechist, at the head of our escort, replied
that we were 'sick people of his household.' 'At
least let them lower their nets,' replied the sentinel.
The bearers were compelled to obey. Fr. Legrand,
who knows the language, was in a blue fright. I, on
the contrary, who did not in the least understand
our danger, thought that we were supposed to get
out, and with joy began to stretch my legs. The
bearers, luckily, did not give me time, but hurriedly
raised us again and trotted on. If the pagans had
paid us a visit what a prize they would have found!
We soon came to the river and found several
Christian junks, into one of which we gladly stepped,
our rowers conveying us safely to the hut of Bishop
Diaz, Vicar Apostolic of the Central Mission of Tong-
king. Two couriers were waiting for us there, sent
by Bishop Retord to escort us to our final destination.
After a few days' rest we bade good-bye to their
cordial, frank, and noble Spanish hospitality, and the

last stage of our journey began, not less dangerous. We went in a junk by night, and had to pass a citadel guarded by four hundred soldiers, stationed there to protect a rice granary belonging to the king. When our boat was opposite the citadel, we were hailed and asked who we were. The owners of the junk replied that we were mandarins. The soldiers did not believe this, and very soon we heard a drum sound the alarm, and in a moment a vessel came after us in hot pursuit. Luckily, we had a favorable wind, and as we were some distance ahead, their boat could not reach us. A second junk was behind us, carrying our baggage and attendants. This they attacked, but our men defended themselves bravely, so that they too escaped. This will give you some idea, dearest sister, of the way in which we travel in Tong-king. One goes generally by night, for greater security; sometimes by water, on rivers or canals, with a continual change of boats; sometimes by land, like mighty lords, in palanquins, or on the backs of slaves in a species of net or hammock, with matting at the side which hides you from the passers-by. Sometimes one can go only on foot, without shoes, in the little narrow paths between the rice-fields. If it be daytime, one has a fair chance of escaping the difficulties of the road, but at night one must be content to walk 'clumpity-clump,' falling into holes one moment, into rice-water the next, unable to find a firm footing anywhere; and often, when you think you are going on swimmingly, your foot slips on the greasy, damp soil, and you measure your length in the mud. Now, don't you think this is a very picturesque way of travelling? I don't say that it is not a little fatiguing now and then, but I assure you it is very laughable at times and gives rise to a host of comical adventures.

TYPICAL JUNKS IN TONG-KING.

"On the 13th of this month we arrived at the scene of our future labors, and I was introduced for the first time to my Vicar Apostolic, the illustrious Bishop Retord, whose name you so often read in the 'Annals.' I found His Grace busy giving a retreat previous to an ordination. Bishop Jeantet, his coadjutor, and Dean of the Tong-king Mission, was helping him. Two other missioners had also arrived on business. We were therefore six Europeans together—two bishops and four missionary priests—a rare event in Tong-king. . . . You can't think how happy I felt to be one of them; there was such frankness and simplicity—such goodness and condescension on the part of our superiors. Very soon we felt as if we had known one another all our lives, and we talked of every conceivable subject—France, Rome, the Russian war, etc.; and before we separated, we sang together a whole heap of new and old songs and national hymns."

Soon after he wrote to Fr. Dallet,—

"Whom do you think I found here with Bishop Retord? Who but my dearest friend, Fr. Theurel, to whom I had said good-bye with such bitter tears only one short year ago. What now of *possibilities,* eh! Father Dallet? Here I have been a month in all the delights of Tong-king, for I assure you there are great pleasures here. Theurel preaches, confesses, burns with desire for work; his health is as good as possible. Mine, perhaps, is not first-rate, but what is the use of complaining? You know the fable, 'Weak health often goes on longest.' So I

8

console myself.   Courage!   I am always repeating
those maxims of St. Teresa's,—

> " 'Let nothing disturb thee!
>   Let nothing affright thee!
>   All passeth away;
>   God only shall stay.
>   Patience wins all;
>   Who hath God needeth nothing,
>   For God is his all.'

" I forgot to tell you that all our worldly goods were
pillaged by the pagans, so that we are destitute of
everything; but what does that signify? He who has
God lacks nothing. You will easily believe that my
first visit was to the tomb of Fr. Bonnard. It is close
to the altar of the College Chapel."

If Fr. Vénard was pleased to find his old friend at
Tong-king, the joy to Fr. Theurel was equally great.
   "Who would ever have said, or thought, or imagined such good fortune!" exclaimed the latter in a
letter to their mutual friend, Father Dallet. "However improbable it may seem, it is nevertheless a positive fact, that here are Father Vénard and I, *together,*
in this western mission of Tong-king, actually in the
same village, in the same house, in the same room!
To describe the pleasure, the joy it has given us! . . .
Yes, but then I feel as if you would break your heart
at not being here too. Nevertheless, you must take
comfort. Will you believe it? Vénard, who has been
here only a month, already speaks the language with
a perfect accent. I think his little voice is made for it.
'All goes well.' I can only wish you the joy and
peace of the poor little Tong-king missioners."

Theophane's happiness in being at last fairly embarked on his work, and in the very mission he would have chosen above all others, found vent in an enthusiastic poem. This outpouring of his heart was occupied with the three great objects of his life: work, the salvation of souls, and death.

CHAPTER X.

Persecutions in Tong-king.

OF all missions those of Cochin-China, Korea, and
Tong-king have been exposed to the cruellest persecutions. Tong-king, perhaps, deserves first rank, and
young missioners have consequently looked upon it
as the vestibule to Heaven. The cross has been the
program of Tong-king missioners; for, from the
first, their lives have been one long martyrdom,—pre-
figured by a great cross found on the Annamite shore
by a Dominican missioner, Diego Advarte, in 1596,
before any European had entered the country.

Jesuits were the founders of the mission, in the
person of Father Alexander Rhodes, who died in
1660. From them it passed into the hands of the
Paris Foreign Mission Seminary, to whose priests it
has always proved a land of special interest. In fact,
from the martyrdom of the first missioner in 1684
until the present day, the Church of Tong-king, always
under the shadow of persecution, may be said to have
grown with her head on the block, and her children's
feet steeped in blood.

Still, there have been moments of calm between the
storms. The first great persecution was in the
eighteenth century, and God avenged it by destroying
its authors and depriving them of their thrones. The
dynasties of Cochin-China and Tong-king were swept

off the face of the earth, and the rightful heir, replaced by the hand of a Christian Bishop, resumed his
sceptre when he had torn asunder the bloody edicts of
the persecutors. Twenty years of peace under this
Prince Gia-Long gave breathing time to the Annamite
Church, and prepared it for the frightful persecutions of Minh-Menh, a monster in human form who
rivalled Nero in his cruelties. The "Annals" narrate
the horrible persecution which broke out in 1833 and
lasted till 1841. Frs. Gagelin, Marchand, Cornay,
Jaccard, Borié, with a great number of Spanish
Dominicans and native teachers, fell victims to this
relentless tyrant. God did not leave him unpunished,
however, for Minh-Menh was killed by a fall from his
horse on the 21st of January, 1841, execrated equally
by pagans and Christians. The new king, Thien-Tri,
weary of the bloody edicts of his predecessor, passed
an act of amnesty, annulling the penal laws. Unfortunately he died in 1848, and was succeeded by Tu-
Duc. During the reign of this prince, famine, cholera,
typhus, and other plagues decimated his people; and
although these trials enabled the Christians to show
themselves in their true colors, and to repay their
persecutors by acts of superhuman charity, still these
calamities were looked on as the result of Divine
vengeance upon the new sect; and the mandarins,
working on the credulity of the people, fanned the
flame of a new persecution, in which, among others,
Frs. Schoeffler and Bonnard were sacrificed. A temporary peace followed, and during this time of comparative security Theophane Vénard arrived.

Notwithstanding all the obstacles thrown in the way
of preaching the Gospel; in spite of the small
numbers of apostolic laborers and the insufficiency of
their resources; in spite of this furious persecution of

Minh-Menh, which lasted twenty years, in no country had Christianity made such wonderful progress as in Tong-king. Bishop Retord wrote at this very time as follows:—

"When I undertook to govern this mission, sixteen years ago, it did not contain more than a hundred thousand Christians. Now there are 140,000, although the cholera of 1851 carried off 10,000. All these converts, with very few exceptions, practise their religion in a way that would shame many Europeans. They are constant attendants at the Sacraments and most diligent in the performance of their religious duties. It is useless to add that they are all Catholics. Heretical ministers, with their wives and children, have never attempted to approach these inhospitable and unhealthful shores, or to face a persecution which can end in only one way—martyrdom."

Bishop Retord was only fifty years old when Theophane Vénard arrived at Tong-king. He was still strong and vigorous, in spite of trials and sufferings. He had established a large seminary of native priests, which numbered upwards of seventy-five, all well instructed and full of zeal for the conversion of their countrymen. The college, which he had erected close to his house, had more than two hundred students, divided into different classes, as in France; while various smaller schools had been established all over the diocese. When the students finished their college terms they passed an examination as catechists. Before receiving his diploma, however, each must have converted at least ten pagans. The theologians were chosen from among the catechists, but were admitted to Holy Orders only after a long and rigorous trial.

The work of God prospered visibly in this land. In the year 1854 fifteen hundred more souls were added to the Christian ranks. Still the number of pagans was enormous, though crowded into a small area.

But let us return to Theophane Vénard. Before his arrival in Tong-king and during his passage, he had suffered from an attack of inflammation of the lungs, which seemed to get worse every day, in spite of the prescriptions of the Chinese physicians. His entire recovery can be attributed only to a direct Divine interposition. The account of it will be found in the following letter to his father, written in March, 1855 :—

"When I wrote to you last, my dearest father, I was with Bishop Retord, at his College of Vinh-Tri. At the end of August, the Bishop sent me to a college in the village of Kê-Doan to study the Annamite language, and associated with me two catechists, who could speak a little Latin. As I had to pass by Kê-non, where there is a seminary directed by Bishop Jeantet, Bishop Retord's coadjutor, I stayed there for eight days. Bishop Jeanet is sixty-three years old, and has been thirty-seven years in the mission. He is a most venerable man, kind and amiable. He was never tired asking me questions about France, that country so dear to the missioner's heart. I was also very much interested in the seminary, and stammered some words of Annamite which I had just learned. From here I left for the college at Lâng-Doân. A month in such study as this went like lightning. On the second Sunday in October I ventured to preach a short sermon in the little church.

The chiefs of the village came to congratulate me,
not that they could understand much of my allocution,
but being Annamites, they are very civil and courteous;
and though I had made such a hash of their language,
they thought it right to compliment me.

"Some days later I fell sick of a pestilential illness
which declared itself in the college. I was one of
its first victims. My catechists nursed me with great
care and attention, and Bp. Retord, Bp. Jeantet, and
Fr. Castex, Pro-Vicar-General of the mission, sent
me all sorts of medicines, which, with the grace of
God, cured me. As soon as I could stand, I went by
boat for a change of air to another village, named
Kè-Dâm, where an Annamite priest has his principal
residence. Remark that I went *in a boat across the
fields,* because every year at this time there is a flood
caused by the overflow of the rivers, the result of the
tropical rains in the western mountains. The whole
country becomes like one vast sea. The villages
themselves are all under water and the only means
of communication is by boats. I found myself well
enough on All Saints' Day to say a low Mass. The
evening before, all the village gathered around the
church to congratulate me on my recovery. The
chiefs, dressed in their best clothes, came to conduct
me solemnly to church, to the sound of native music
and repeated hurrahs. You see, dearest father, that
the Annamites care for their missioners. But the
evening of the Feast of All Saints was the reverse
of the medal. I had hardly gone to bed when they
came to wake me, and to announce the arrival of a
mandarin for a domiciliary visit. They were in a
great fright and implored me to go on to another
village. Though the news was not very certain, I
thought that I had better comply with their wishes,

and so packed up my traps as fast as I could. I was
carried with all my little establishment on men's
backs in the middle of the night to the said village.
This was my first nocturnal flight; since then I have
had many others! I remained eight days in the house
of a devout Christian in this place, who acted as if
he could not make enough of me; and to show my
gratitude I made a great distribution of medals and
rosaries. Then I went on to a college in the little
town of Hoâng-Nguyén, where Fr. Castex has his
principal residence. Fr. Castex was on a diocesan
tour and would not return till December. I was,
therefore, the only European in the college, at the
head of which was a native priest, an Annamite Father.
Here I began to hear confessions, first among the
students, and then among the Christians of the village; but I made little or no progress, because very
soon I fell sick again with inflammation of the lungs,
which endangered my life. But I recovered. Fr.
Castex returned with Fr. Titaud, and then another
of our missioners, Fr. Néron, came along, so that we
were four altogether. You can fancy what a pleasure
it was! After some days of mutual enjoyment, Fr.
Titaud went back to his district. Fr. Néron also
prepared to leave for his College of Vinh-Tri, of
which he is the superior; but he was taken prisoner
in crossing the river and very nearly gave us a fresh
martyr. By a special providence, the soldier who
had hastened to the village to get a reinforcement in
order to secure our poor brother, met the chief of the
canton, who knew Fr. Néron and had a great regard
for him; although a pagan, he connived at his escape
and the only loss was a sum of money.

"You want to know more about my health. On
New Year's day I was so ill that I could hardly re-

ceive the visits of congratulation from the Christians
of the district. The bishop sent me his own physician,
a very clever man, whose medicines did me some
good, but after his departure I fell ill again. Fr.
Castex took every possible care of me and was extremely anxious on my account. I was obliged to give
up confessing, saying Mass, or Office, even reading
and writing, and I was scarcely allowed to speak at
all. At last Fr. Castex advised me to make a novena
to the Sacred Hearts of Jesus and Mary, and insisted
on sharing it with me. We began on the day of the
Purification and at once I felt myself getting better;
since then all bad symptoms have disappeared and my
strength has nearly returned. To the Sacred Hearts
of Jesus, Mary, and Joseph be the praise.

"About this time the political horizon darkened; a
revolutionary party broke out in Tong-king; a new
edict, emanating from the king, denounced our holy
religion; evil-disposed persons betrayed to the mandarins the residences of the missioners; the College
of Kê-Vinh was broken up; and Bishop Retord, with
several of his missioners, had to keep himself in
hiding. The mandarin of Kê-Cho, the capital of Tong-
king, laid siege to the Seminary of Kê-Non, but Bishop
Jeantet had already taken flight to the mountains,
whence he wrote to Fr. Castex and me: 'I have been
looking up my old haunts, and the caves where I lived
at the time of the persecution of Minh-Menh,—not
that it is very easy for an old man like me to scramble
up and down rocks and precipices. I sometimes wonder how I manage to get on at all.'

"The mandarin found only an Annamite Father and
a deacon, whom he released soon after, although not

without the payment of 10,000 francs. The College
of Kê-Non is at least still standing.

"As for Fr. Castex and myself, after having been
chased from one village to another, we have finally
taken refuge in a convent near the town of Bùt-Dông,
where we have lived as hermits with two catechists
for the last two months. Very soon, however, I hope
we shall be able to show our faces again, as the storm
seems to have subsided. Yet we must be prudent,
for the denouncer of Bishop Jeantet, having failed
to catch him, has offered his own head to the mandarin
if he cannot deliver a European into his hands before
the end of the year. Everyone, therefore, keeps himself on guard. What will happen, God knows; in any
case it is better to hope than to fear. Bishop Retord
writes to us, 'Jesus and Mary will not abandon us
now any more than they have done before. Pray
then with great confidence, and do not let us be discouraged or give way to sadness. If any of us win
the martyr's palm so much the better. *Sicut fuerit
voluntas tua, sic fiat.*'†

"The rebellion goes on spreading; it wants to re-
establish the ancient dynasty on the throne, and the
revolutionists say that they will soon present the new
king. On the other hand the misery is very great.
Last year's rice harvest was bad enough; this year
in many places it is simply lost. Thousands of people
are dying of hunger. It is enough to move any one
to compassion. People in Europe have no idea of the
common misery in this unhappy country. The feasts
of the New Year, which are generally so gay, have
this season passed in sadness and mourning, and it is

---

† Be it done according to Thy will.

not probable that the end of the year will be brighter. Now, dearest father, I must stop. Adieu. Do not be anxious about me. *What God keeps is well kept.* Stay well; pray for me; and may the joy of our Lord Jesus Christ fill your heart forevermore."

CHAPTER XI.

Labors and Trials.

UP to this time Theophane had not said much of his relations with the people. He filled up this void in the following letter to his sister: —

"You say you would like to be a little bird, my dearest sister, and see how I get on with my new children. Well, I assure you I begin to love them very much. The Annamite people are thoroughly good and their respect for the missioners is very great. Until now the state of the country and my small acquaintance with the language have prevented my doing much, but the principal people of the villages often come to see me and bring some little present. I could only say a few unintelligible sentences at first, which I saw made them very much inclined to laugh; but they would not have done so for all the world, they are so afraid of hurting my feelings. Very often the peasants come to pay me a visit: one day it is the father of a family who has married off one of his children and brings me a pig's head killed for the feast; another day some mother arrives who wishes to recommend her son just starting for the army; or four or five poor women will come together to offer me a little basket of fruit, or to ask me for a rosary or a cross. I can answer only in a few words but every one goes away pleased and satisfied. It is the custom among the Annamites that no one shall present himself to a superior without offering a present. If our poor

Christians ever have any fine fruit, or extra good fish, or any vegetable larger than usual, they take the greatest delight in coming to offer it to the missioners. I assure you, Mélanie, I love the Annamites very much, and I thank God every day that He has consecrated me to their service. All is not, certainly, *colour de rose,* but there will always be thorns in every path.

"One word as to these nuns of Tong-king, about whom you make such eager inquiries. They are natives living in community under the authority of an abbess; they do not take vows and are received very young. They work in the fields, prepare the cotton for linen cloths, or *sell pills,* which will astonish you, and probably make you laugh; but it is by this means that they gain access to pagan children who are ill and baptize those in danger of death.

"They live poorly, pray a great deal, give themselves the discipline, and fast far more than ordinary Christians. When necessary they act as couriers to carry letters from one mission to another, in which capacity they are often invaluable; there is nothing in this occupation which shocks the feelings or customs of their country. On such occasions they always go in pairs. They often carry great loads, but they are accustomed to toil and fatigue, as all Annamite women are. The Christians always call them *'Sisters,'* and they are universally loved and respected.

"It is very pleasant to hear the native prayers, especially when they are said well together; their harmony has often touched me more than the most beautiful European music. The people have some very pretty litanies of Our Lady, especially one of the Immaculate Conception. But their acts of thanksgiving after Communion are the most touching; when I hear them, it moves me almost to tears. The Annamites do not know how to pray in silence or in a low voice; and even if there is only one communicant, he intones his thanksgiving aloud, either alone or in company with the choir. The catechists sing the plain chant very well, and sometimes chant High Mass; but then there is always a musical accompaniment. Their instruments are the violin, harp, drums, fife, and cymbals. They have not much variety in their music, and during High Mass will play a single tune over and over till one is satiated with it. But after all, God is, perhaps, as much praised and glorified by this simple, devout congregational music as by the most magnificent harmony, executed by first-class artists. It is the vibration of the heart, and not of the chords, which is acceptable to Him.

"And my Latin scholars, you ask, are they very learned? It is difficult for them to be, since they have no dictionaries. At the end of their studies they understand the Catechism of the Council of Trent, and of late years Bishop Retord has started a class of Philosophy which is conducted in Latin. You may well imagine that we do not trouble our heads to teach Ovid, Horace, or heathen mythology to these poor Annamites. Hence the controversy as to the classics must be judged by itself."

In a letter to an old friend about this time we find a touching passage showing the simplicity and *naïveté* of these people in their religious rites:—

"I am quite sure that your first experience in performing a marriage ceremony was widely different from mine. In Tong-king there are no marriage processions and no bridesmaids, as in France. The married couple receive the sacrament as they do the Blessed Eucharist without any demonstration. Well, my *fiancés* having been to confession, and thus prepared themselves, the day was fixed. I went very early in the morning, and sang Mass for the whole population (they keep early hours in Tong-king). Then my catechist made a signal for the young couple —each was about eighteen years of age—to go up to the altar. The young girl mounted the steps; but where was her betrothed? He never appeared. After waiting some time in vain, the poor child was quietly told to go back, and come again at the same time to-morrow. Resigned and gentle, she obeyed. The next day the future husband made his appearance at the proper moment and I blessed the marriage. In the course of the day the newly-married couple, conducted by the sister of the bride, came to pay me a visit, and to thank me. I ventured to ask why the young gentleman had not made his appearance the first day. He answered with perfect simplicity, that he 'did not wake in time.'"

We cannot better describe the people and the life of the young missioner, than by his letters, which are graphic pictures of his daily trials and their consolations. In September, 1855, Theophane wrote again to his family:—

"I hope that my last letters, written in March, have reached you. Since then it has pleased God to throw me again on a bed of sickness. On Ash Wednesday I went to Father Castex, Vicar-General of the mission, who was at the College of Hoàng-Nguyên. The distance was not more than a quarter of a league but the road was full of mud and water. I took a violent chill and fever, and from that moment I got worse and worse. I was also obliged to flee by night several times from the mandarins and hide in the rice-fields.

This did not mend matters. The people around me thought the end was at hand and prepared everything for my funeral. But God sent me a doctor, who gave me some new sort of medicine which brought me to life again. I received Extreme Unction twice, and each time God was pleased, in strengthening my soul, to restore my body. I am now staying at Kê-Vinh with Bishop Retord, who hopes to complete my cure; but I am afraid it will be difficult, as my left lung is almost gone. I have terrible perspirations and an oppression on my chest; in the morning I sometimes have such violent expectoration and running at the nose that I cannot say Mass. On the other hand my appetite is good, so that I can go on with my little studies. Do not let my illness make you unhappy, my dearly-loved people! but pray for me, that the sufferings of my body may be for the spiritual welfare of my soul. . . . "

In this September letter he alludes as follows to the persecutions:—

"They threatened to be terrible; but thank God! our worst apprehensions have not been realized. Our purses have suffered most; for one could close the mandarins' mouths only by bars of silver. Our poor missions have indeed been bled to satisfy pagan rapacity. These poor Annamites are always the victims of some misfortune or some act of oppression. One year an inundation comes; the next, a drought. The harvest almost always fails. A bowl of rice is all that the people want, and even this much they cannot always obtain. Yet these rapacious gentlemen, the mandarins, who are nominally their fathers and protectors, think of nothing but pillage and robbery, and how to suck wealth out of these

9

unhappy people like so many leeches. I really believe there is no such thing as an honest man among the mandarins. The Christians are a capital bank for them; their religion being proscribed by the king, it is the easiest thing in the world to accuse them at any moment of 'treason and rebellion against the state.' From the village mayors up to the mandarin governors of the provinces, every man will have his share in the plunder. In a village which is half Christian and half pagan, the Christians pay a heavy ransom to have liberty of conscience. . . . . This year we have had no martyrdom. I have heard of a doctor and his two brothers who were thrown into prison by the mandarin and who are still in captivity. I know this physician; he is a most fervent and excellent man, and has already been a Confessor for the Faith in the Minh-Menh persecution. Thanks to the interposition of a friendly mandarin at court, Bishop Retord has been able to return to his college; and Bishop Jeantet has also gone back to his seminary. So after the storm comes the calm, and God protects His own. Since January I have not had a line from any of you and am getting rather anxious for tidings. May God and His Holy Mother preserve you, my dearest father, and sister, and brothers, from all evil, now and forevermore!"

A little later he writes:—

"I am dying out like a candle, and holding to life by a mere thread. I think the doctors have given me up but I can still rejoice in whatever God appoints. Perhaps this is the last note you will receive from me. Pray for me, that, though my poor body perishes from day to day, my soul may be saved through the merits

THE VÉNARD HOME AT ST. LOUP,
where the martyr was born.

of Him Who died for me. We shall meet one another in a brighter and better home. Adieu!"

On the 1st of December he wrote again to his sister, saying that he had recovered his strength; that his left side was much better; and that she must join with him in thanking and praising God for having so unexpectedly restored him to health. He continues:—

"We are in a period of comparative peace, so that our schools are re-opened. The bishop can officiate pontifically on festivals; and we may go, *in the daytime,* to walk in the college gardens—a favor of which you would understand the magnitude better if you had been confined, like us, for so long a time in one room, without daring either to sing or speak above a whisper. Lately the government has been put in a state of excitement by the appearance of an English man-of-war at Touranne, which is close to the capital of the kingdom in Cochin-China. I believe that the Governor General of Hong-Kong and the Plenipotentiaries of Queen Victoria came to propose a treaty of commerce to Tu-Duc, the Annamite king. However, this 'gracious sovereign' would not receive the despatches; so the English had to retire without doing anything. But the consequences have been rather disastrous for us, as they choose to fancy that we sent for the English. We have had no news from home for more than a year. I try to be patient but each courier who arrives and brings no letters is a fresh mortification. Pray for me, that I may strive to live above all these feelings and become a more worthy priest of Jesus Christ; so that in the difficult post which I now occupy, I may have the necessary grace and prudence. As for me, I never cease to pray for you all. Remember your poor little Theophane!"

At this time the Crimean war and the proclamation of the dogma of the Immaculate Conception occupied the minds of men of every class in Europe. Although sixteen months had elapsed since Theophane had received any letters from home, yet the news of these two great events reached our missioners and rejoiced their sad hearts. Theophane wrote to express his joy to his sister, and adds:—

"Since my last letter the persecution has been renewed and one of our native priests, Huông, has been martyred. This did not prevent Bishop Retord from preaching his Lenten missions, and, thanks to Our Lady's protection, we have not had to take many more precautions than usual. As far as I am concerned, I had the pleasure of accompanying His Grace in one of his diocesan tours, where the work was arduous and incessant. He celebrated the Offices of Holy Week and Easter at Kê-Vinh before an immense congregation, and everything passed off well, and in comparative peace, if such a word can be used in connection with people in our position. You will perhaps wonder how, being continually on the *'qui vive,'* and in hiding, with a price put upon our heads, we can think of keeping feasts and talk of peace. But it seems as if a special protection of God and the Blessed Virgin rested upon us, so that we may 'serve Him without fear.' Besides, when we do get a little liberty, we set it against the continual vexations and constraints to which we are generally subject. We are like rats coming out for a little bite, regardless of the cat, and hastening to regain our holes on the first alarm or sound of danger."

At last, after a nineteen months' *fast,* the poor missioners received their letters from home. Theophane then wrote:—

"On the feast of St. Peter, Bishop Retord called in all his missioners and his coadjutor, Bishop Jeantet, to meet him at the College of Kê-Vinh. We made a retreat in common, and passed fifteen days in the most perfect calm and peace, in spite of the emissaries of the mandarins who were spying in the neighborhood. We sang heaps of French songs and enjoyed ourselves thoroughly. Just before we parted, a courier arrived from Cochin-China, bringing news from Europe of the allies' success, the proclamation of peace, the birth of the Prince Imperial, and the rejoicings of the people at the new dogma. We were told also of the embassy sent by the Emperor to negotiate with the Annamite king, so as to stop the persecution of Christians, and especially of the French missioners, whose blood this king, a worthy successor of his father, has so cruelly shed. We were about to disperse to our respective missions and had already taken leave of one another, when a tremendous inundation came, worse than any in the memory of the oldest inhabitant, and it compelled us to stay where we were. The flood lasted a whole month and the waters covered four large provinces, besides breaking down the dykes in many places. The newly-sown rice was completely lost; that which was almost ready for the harvest was submerged, and the greater portion rotted; many villages were destroyed, and thousands of persons drowned, or killed by the falling of the mud walls of their houses. Many took refuge in the mountains; others huddled close to the dykes which had resisted the rush of waters, and remained

there without food for days; others again, like ourselves, were kept prisoners in their houses, obliged
to battle with the ever-rising flood. Often it was
necessary to take up the flooring and make a temporary standing-ground in the upper story or close
under the roof, which had to be pierced to give air.

"In the villages where inundations are an annual
occurrence, there is a system of boats, which are kept
ready in case of need, but in other places you can
imagine the misery! Besides, the gardens are all
destroyed, trees killed, and cattle and domestic animals
drowned. As for ourselves, the students of the
college, by working day and night, contrived to build
a dyke sufficiently strong to protect the church
and our place of refuge, but the bishop's house was
full of water. In the midst of this I fell sick of a
violent fever with an attack of asthma, and it was in
one of the worst fits that your letter was brought to
me and acted like the dew on the parched ground.
Don't fancy that this is a figure of speech. I do
assure you it is a fact that the sight of your hand-
writing, and the joy that I felt, reacted on my whole
system, and the fever was sensibly diminished. However, just as I was beginning to rejoice in a kind of
convalescence, I caught typhoid fever, which again
brought me to the very gates of death. Bishop Retord
and my fellow-missioners said Masses for me to St.
Peter of Alcantara (to whom, St. Teresa says, our
Lord refuses nothing), and I got better from that
time. The end of all this succession of fevers is, that
although I am about again, I am still very weak; but
as my appetite has returned, I hope to be able to work
soon. My left side no longer gives me so much pain;

and as God has preserved me until now, I hope that He will do so to the end, and enable me to do something for His glory before I die."

After receiving these letters, his family naturally feared that the following courier would bring the news of his death. Their surprise and joy were therefore very great at the contents of a letter, dated June, 1857, in which he says, "At the end of the year 1856 every one thought I was dying. So I took the advice of Bishop Retord and consented to try a Chinese remedy, which is used only in extreme cases, and is called, in Annamite, '*Phep-Quenou.*' In Europe it would be considered a species of cauterization. It consists in applying little burning balls of a certain herb, something like absinthe, to different parts of the body. There are, the Chinese doctors say, three hundred and sixty points in the human body which may thus be burnt. The difficulty is to know which is the right spot; otherwise, you may be lamed, or become blind, or have your mouth drawn to one side, etc., etc. I was burnt in five hundred different places, about two hundred of which were near the lungs. At the end of a few days these cauterizations, or inoculations, produced a little yellow pustule full of matter; this is a sign that the operation has been successful, as the system is supposed thus to reject all that is noxious. The result has been that I am wonderfully better, and my patience in enduring this small purgatory for several hours has been rewarded. But enough of my wretched ailings, for to be sick is natural to me; and Bishop Retord declares that I have chosen sufferings for my specialty.

"I would rather talk to you about the state of our poor mission. We were at Kê-Vinh in February,

when one Monday, at eight o'clock, one of the villagers
came in hot haste to tell us that the mandarin of the
southern province had surrounded the village and
was coming to seize us. Bishop Retord was forced
by the students into a subterranean hiding-place;
Father Charbonnier and I were stuffed into a place
between two walls, where we remained for four hours
without seeing the light of day. At the end of this
time, some one came to announce to us that the
domiciliary visit was over, and the mandarin gone;
but that he had carried off with him the director of
the college (a venerable priest named Tinh), one of
the catechists, and the mayor of the place. The
truth was, that in the neighboring province certain
Christians had been forced by blows to reveal the
bishop's residence; and a poor woman, who was the
bearer of some European letters to one of our
missioners, was seized, and, being put to the torture,
confessed in her agony, that they were destined for
the College of Kê-Vinh. But this was only the beginning of a series of misfortunes. In March the mandarin returned with two hundred soldiers to destroy
both the church and the college; but we had received
warning in time, and had all taken refuge in the
mountains. The next day we returned to find everything in ruins, and as we were surrounded by spies,
it was thought best to leave the place for a time. I
went by night, secretly, in a boat, to my old quarters
at Hoàng-Nguyên, while Bishop Retord and Father
Charbonnier returned to their hiding-places in the
mountains. Father Castex and Father Theurel, the
superior of the college, were at Hoàng when I
arrived; but the former was soon seized with rheu-
matic fever, and became dangerously ill. Bishop
Retord, hearing of this, came down from the hills to

administer the last consolations to our dear friend
and brother, who expired on the eve of Trinity, after
great sufferings. His death was, however, perfectly
peaceful, and he slept the sleep of the just. To me,
who had lived in great intimacy with him for two
years, the loss is very great, and I have scarcely
courage to face the future. Bishop Retord has given
me his post, for which I feel utterly unworthy. May
I only imitate the holiness of my predecessor and win
as many souls for our dear Master as he did!

"Our good old priest, Tinh, of whom I spoke as
having been carried off by the persecutor, made a
glorious confession of faith, and was instantly beheaded. The Christians had no time to help him in
his last moments, but he was one who kept his lamp
always burning. The sword of the executioner broke
in halves during the operation. The mandarins
thought this a bad omen, and in consequence offered
pagan sacrifices to appease the dead ancestors of
the victim. Poor Tinh's three companions, having
also generously confessed the faith, were condemned
to perpetual banishment in a distant, unhealthful
mountain. A few months later, a pagan prefect,
having taken a spite against Bishop Diaz, a Dominican,
denounced him to the mandarins, and his Lordship was
seized at his residence in the village of Biù-Chu and
dragged to the prefecture, where he is now imprisoned
and rigorously guarded. We expect every day to hear
that he has been condemned to death. The great
mandarin has a special hatred for all Christians just
now, and has placed crosses at the gates of the town,
so that everyone going out or coming in shall
trample them under foot. The unhappy Christians
have been subject to domiciliary visits day and night.
Fortunately, however, they were warned in time, and

the greater number have taken flight. In Cochin-China the state of things is still worse.

"I told you, in a previous letter, that the Emperor was going to send a plenipotentiary to plead the cause of the Christians with the Annamites. Well, M. de Montigny arrived in due time, but with only two little steamers and a small warship, and with no real powers to treat. So the king refused to hear him and the Frenchmen had to weigh anchor and go. The people, Christians and pagans, who had been rejoicing at the prospect of being delivered from the tyrants, seeing the complete failure, were not only thoroughly discouraged, but began to despise a power which could do nothing, and this shame has fallen heavily on us poor missioners. If France meddles at all, she ought to do it thoroughly, so as to carry her point. Still, all hope is not gone, as the Chinese war has brought a large fleet into these waters. M. de Montigny, unable to help us as he wished, threatened the king with the account which he would have to render for the French blood shed in his dominions. The king, seeing the interest which M. de Montigny took in the Christian missioners, imagined that we had sent for him; so that when M. de Montigny went away he left us in the claws of a tiger more than ever irritated against us. In consequence, they seized a Christian mandarin with thirty of his neophytes, and after having made them suffer horrible tortures, condemned them to be beheaded. Then the poor mandarin was dragged through all the streets of the capital, and at each corner his sentence was read out, while he received thirty blows with a stick. This sentence was full of blasphemies against our Lord such as these: 'The Christians pretend that those who suffer tortures are sure of Paradise after their death. Who knows that? Fools that they are! If it were so, why does not their Jesus come and deliver them?' Oh, my Lord! Thou hast heard their words, and wilt remember them. Yes, I have a firm conviction that Thou wilt aid us and avenge Thy name!"

After the death of Fr. Castex, as we have said, Fr. Vénard remained at the College of Hoàng-Nguyèn, where he had the joy of being once more with his great friend, Fr. Theurel. But the difficulty of carrying on the work of the missions, owing to the violence of the persecution, weighed heavily on his mind. "I sometimes ask myself," he writes, 'Is God's grace no longer so effective as before? Has the time passed for the conversion of the Gentiles? Or are we poor missioners less zealous than our predecessors?' It is quite heart-breaking to look around and to see nothing but heathen pagodas, to hear nothing but the bells of the bonzes, to witness only diabolical processions! Our dear Lord has to bow before the ministers of Buddha and Confucius. His missioners live in holes and caverns and a price is put upon their heads. Is not the day of their deliverance at hand? In this Annamite kingdom the penal laws are most cruel and rigid, but they are only half carried out, on account of the greed of mandarins, who simply use them as a means to extort money. If at least one might buy peace with the money! But no; this half and half persecution undoes everything. One day you build a church, open a school, establish a college. The next week perhaps you have to flee and your works are all destroyed. Another time you pay a large sum to a mandarin to be left in peace. Then he goes out of office, and another comes, who perhaps asks double the price, which it is impossible to raise;

and the edifice you have reared with such pains and labor crumbles away! As for me, I have no hope but in God and in His Immaculate Mother, whose Conception has just been so gloriously proclaimed. Under the yoke of the oppressor, we are like the Jewish captives, 'Super flumina Babylonis.' But I look on this proclamation as a rainbow, which is to announce to us the end of the storm."

In September, 1857, he wrote again to his sister,—

"My Dearest Sister,—You will have seen by my last letter that my health is improved, and that Bishop Retord has given me a new district. I have upwards of twelve thousand Christians here, divided into four large parishes, with six or seven native priests under me. My duty is to go from parish to parish, seeing that all is in good order; establish peace if there should be discord; give the necessary dispensations; confirm, in cases where the Bishop or Vicar Apostolic cannot come to perform that sacramental function; give retreats and missions; in fact, strive to augment in all hearts the love of God and the zeal for His Church. As to the pagans, I have never counted them, but there must be from 250,000 to 300,000. It needs ten St. Francis Xaviers to bring all these people to the knowledge of the Gospel. At this moment it is difficult for us to do much in the way of conversion on account of the violence of the persecution. Still from time to time souls are garnered. When the children are ill, the mothers bring them for baptism. The other day a young widow brought her little one who was dying. She herself was in the greatest misery, having eaten only five times in twelve days. I baptized her child, and then entrusted her to the care of one of our

Christian women, who is now preparing the mother likewise for that holy sacrament.

"After the Feast of the Assumption I went to a district almost entirely pagan. Only about two hundred Christians were scattered here and there. It was close to the residence of the mandarin. No European had ever penetrated so far into the interior; so I had to keep myself as hidden as I possibly could. But the children whom I had confirmed, unintentionally betrayed me by chattering and saying 'A little European has come into the village, very small, but very white and pretty;' for you must know, my dear little sister, that we poor Europeans pass for great beauties, and one who is considered dark in France appears white among these people, who are burnt a mahogany color by the tropical sun. Well, what was to be done? The hare was started and the dogs on the scent! I resolved not to lose courage; but putting my whole trust in God, I worked day and night in this, His neglected vineyard, during one whole week; meanwhile the Christians, who were in a terrible fright, acted as sentinels, and refused all visitors whose curiosity prompted them to wish to have a look at the European. Having finished my work, I departed secretly by night, favored by the darkness, and came to another place, where the villagers, amounting to four or five thousand souls, were all Christians, and the neighborhood, though pagan, was favorable to Christianity.

"My goings and comings are easy at this season of the year, as the inundations last for four or five months. The country becomes an immense sea, in which float green villages. There are no roads. Everyone goes in boats; but fortunately there are plenty of these in all shapes and sizes. I have one which holds just one person. It is very light, and

woven of bamboo; every evening, sitting like a
tailor in my little skiff, I paddle myself along to my
different penitents, often meeting one or the other on
the way, and then having races to see who shall be
the quickest, in which manœuvre I need not say that
your poor brother is always beaten. I make a point
of visiting my flock in their own homes, which gives
them immense pleasure. In fact, it is impossible to
find a better-disposed people than these poor Annamites, or to meet more fervent or pious souls. This
year (and last) the inundations have been extraordinary, and more than a foot of water came into my
house. I had fishes, frogs and toads, crabs and ser-
pents, swimming about my room very happily, while
I myself was perched on some planks about three or
four inches above them. But what I disliked most was
that the rats insisted upon taking refuge on my mat,
and one night I squashed one while I was asleep. It
was a disagreeable discovery, but on waking, I found
a poisonous viper, with black and white stripes, which
had likewise coiled itself up on my poor bed, as if to
ask for hospitality, and was hissing just as I stretched
my toes. So I forgave the rat. However, I determined, under the circumstances, to raise my house. I
got the Christians to bring me a quantity of earth, and
then to lift up my house four or five feet. For you
must know that this house, like all the rest, consists
only of two or three wooden columns, interlaced with
bamboo trellice, outside of which is a thin plaster of
mud, covered with a coating of lime that is supposed
to look 'grand.' The height is never more than ten
or fifteen feet, and the roof is made of dry leaves.
The whole edifice is easy enough to transport, as it is
very light, and a man can lift it in his hand. So now
I am high and dry, and away from the water. I

have actually made a little garden, with flower seeds
from Europe, and I have a rose tree, a honeysuckle,
some balsams, and some stocks. Don't you think
I was very persevering? But now, my darling little
Mélanie, don't go and imagine, in your foolish, loving
sister's heart, that I am a great saint. I am not
even a little wee one! Sickness has weakened my
poor body, and stupefied my senses, and cooled my
ardor. You see I own all my spiritual miseries to you
so that you may pity me and pray for me. My
heart is as cold and icy sometimes as the tropical sun
is burning and hot. There are no beautiful churches
or services here to rouse one's tepidity, and to drop
a little dew of piety on one's frigid soul. Pray then
for me, dearest sister, that the heavenly dew may
descend and soften your brother's heart; that his
interior life may be strengthened, and his prayers
become more fervent, and the spirit of sacrifice more
entire; so that he who bears the great title of missioner may do works worthy of the name. Ask also
that God may give me a little more health and
strength, for you know how the body reacts on the
soul; and if the laborer stumbles in tracing the furrow,
it will be crooked and only half done. Beg the
Author of all Good for these gifts which I so greatly
need, that His work may be better done, and His
name be glorified.

"You ask me if I should not like some object of
devotion, or something for my church. If you could
manage to make me a chasuble I should be most
grateful, and my catechists would be delighted. Only
yesterday they said to me, 'Oh, father, do write to
France, and get a prettier set of vestments for Mass
on Feast Days.'

"And now, dearest sister, God bless and keep you and all near and dear to us. I recommend myself especially to the prayers of all who care for your unworthy brother,

Theophane."

CHAPTER XII.

Under Fire.

THE letters written by Theophane Vénard in May, 1858, did not reach their destination, and to follow the course of events preceding his martyrdom, we must have recourse to the report of Bishop Retord.

"Our position," the Bishop wrote at this time, "is terrible. We are like birds on the branch of a tree, always on the alert, always receiving messages saying that we have been discovered by the spies, that we have been denounced, that the mandarins are surrounding our mission, and that such and such Christians have been pillaged, tortured, and put to death on our account. In order to spare them, we hide in our little boats, or in caverns, or in tombs in the mountains, where we run the risk of being buried alive. One day we had to remain in one of these tombs for eight hours, being able to breathe only through a bamboo tube. When we came out we were all like idiots, and only half conscious. But the bodily pains we endure are nothing to the anguish of our souls, lest any neophytes should deny their faith under torture. The searchings of the mandarins are so thorough, that it is almost impossible to escape. One of our native priests was seized last week and thrown into prison, from which he was released only by martyrdom. His companions and pupils, who had been arrested at the same time, were condemned to

10

perpetual exile. Among them was a little child ten
years old who, rather than renounce Jesus Christ, bore
the strokes of the bastinado, and after being separated from his parents and home, was sentenced
to wear till death the malefactor's chain. Another
priest and a catechist were arrested the next day and
gained the martyr's palm.

"Two new edicts fulminated against us have greatly
kindled the zeal and fury of the pagan governors.
Our chapels are destroyed, our houses demolished,
our students dispersed, and our money wasted in vain
attempts to redeem our converts. There is not one
of my poor missioners who has not his personal
troubles besides. Frs. Theurel and Vénard, surrounded by their trembling, weeping flock, have been
obliged to take refuge in subterranean caverns, where
the mandarins as yet have been unable to follow them.
Fr. Titaud saw his church and house destroyed before
his eyes, and hid himself with difficulty in a wild
solitude, exposed to the attacks of all kinds of
venomous creatures. The same has happened to Fr.
Saiget. Fr. Mathevon, hard pressed, nearly fell into
the hands of the enemy, who had already seized his
catechist and his guide. It suddenly occurred to him
to throw himself between two or three old mats and
he thus escaped detection. Bishop Jeantet has had
to stop his theological class and hide in the mountains;
God knows when he will be able to return to his post.
Even Fr. Charbonnier and I, who hoped to have
escaped the storm in my little retreat of Vinh-Tri,
have had to seek shelter (which men denied us) of
the bears and tigers who have their holes in the
rocks. Frs. Galy and Néron, who are at the extremity
of the mission, have enjoyed a certain immunity until

BISHOP THEUREL, OF TONG-KING,
Confessor of the Faith.

now, but I expect every day to hear of fresh disasters."

Then follows a recital of the tortures to which the Christians were exposed, to compel them to apostatize. We give a brief *resumé* of these.

The most ordinary instrument of torture is the "cangue." It is a species of ladder, four or five feet long, and varying in weight from ten to forty pounds, the two sides of which are united at a width of six inches by four iron bars. The head of the martyr is passed through the middle bars, and the two heavy sides rest on the shoulders. To bear this day and night is absolute misery. The flesh of the neck and shoulders becomes raw; and when the inhuman jailers drag the sufferers from side to side, the agony may be imagined.

In the prison itself, which is a species of hell upon earth, a fresh torture is resorted to. This is a kind of stocks, in which the feet are caught just above the ankle; very often these are too tight, and enter the flesh. What makes the stocks more insupportable is the fact that innumerable bugs live in the cracks of the wood, and constantly suck the blood of the victims. These stocks being immovable, the unhappy prisoners are compelled to remain in the same position day and night, either sitting or crouching, without being able to move in the least.

The third torture, and one universally employed, is the "rotin" or knout, which is inflicted most brutally. Several victims are laid flat on their stomachs in rows, one after the other, the feet of one being fastened to the hands of the next, and all so stretched as almost to dislocate their joints. Each blow inflicted produces blood, and gives an involuntary start to all like an electric shock, so that those who are not

struck suffer nearly as much as those who are; and as
a certain interval is left between the strokes, the
torment lasts for several hours, each sufferer receiving fifty or sixty blows. The instrument used
for this horrible flagellation is a flexible whip, about
the thickness of one's little finger, and nearly four
feet long. The lash is split into four bits, firmly
tied with twine steeped in gum, which renders the
blow heavier and prevents its being softened in
striking.

After the flagellation come the pincers, either cold
or heated in a forge, the bellows of which are always
going, so that the pincers may be red hot. A portion
of the martyr's flesh is seized with the iron, then
dragged and torn off with a rapid twist of the pincers,
while the victim is tightly bound to the ground. This
operation is renewed on the same individual five or
six times. The agony inflicted by the pincers when
cold is more intense, but the wound is more easily
healed than is that produced by the red hot pincers.
In the latter case the flesh around the burn generally
festers, and the whole process apparently poisons the
blood; but the pain is less, because the burning
deadens the nerves.

A fifth torture consists in forcing the confessor to
kneel on a piece of wood full of nails, the sharp
points of which pierce the flesh and penetrate to the
bone. The unhappy victim sighs pitifully during this
protracted torture, while the mandarins laugh at his
contortions, and add to his agonies by their fearful
blasphemies against our Lord.

If the martyr has survived the infliction of all these
horrors, the persecutors try a sixth method of
torture, which consists of dragging him by his
"cangue" to the cross, while they scourge him, striving

to compel him to trample it under his feet. If his lips still move in prayer, the executioners strike him on the mouth, and offer insult in the most disgusting manner to the object of his veneration.

Then the unhappy victims are again thrown into prison, heavily ironed, and separated one from the other. The chains which they wear are of three pieces, one being fastened around the neck by a large ring, the other two around the ankles by smaller rings, soldered to prevent the possibility of their being undone. These chains weigh five or six pounds. If the chain is too long the prisoner must hold it in his hand to be able to walk. If too short, his back is constantly bent. After tortures like these, it is not surprising if the courage of the Christians should sometimes, though very seldom, fail, and these occasional apostasies add to the sorrow of the missioner, whose whole moral nature has been agonized by the sight of such sufferings.

Bishop Retord declared that his sadness was intense, and that only the special grace of God could enable him to bear such misery. From Easter Day, 1858, nothing but misfortunes overwhelmed his diocese, and he gives a short summary of them in a letter to Admiral Rigault de Genouilly, who had written to ask him for some account of the state of things. After a graphic picture of the persecution, the Bishop adds, "And now you ask what has become of us poor missioners, apostles in a field once so fertile, now so desolate and abandoned? I can hardly tell you. It is more than six months since I have received news of Fr. Néron, and I do not know where he is, or if he still lives. Fr. Galy started on an Annamite merchant-ship to implore the aid of the Spaniards in Manila; but what has become of him I do not know.

I fear that he may have been assassinated at sea like Fr. Salgot. Frs. Titaud, Theurel, and Vénard, finding themselves surrounded by the enemy in their little bamboo huts, escaped by night and took to the mountains. It is more than two months since I have had any tidings of them. Bishop Jeantet, after wandering about in the hills for a long time, took refuge with some faithful peasants; and being obliged to escape in the night, was nearly drowned crossing a river.

"I have no news whatever of Fr. Saiget. As for Frs. Charbonnier, Mathevon, and myself, who have been at Bût-Sôn since the 13th of June, we have been living as best we could,—one day in a peasant's cabin, the next under the trees, or in the bushes, or scrambling over impassable roads, exposed to a burning sun or torrents of rain. We are half dead from hunger, with scarcely any clothes to cover us, overwhelmed with fatigue and sorrow, not knowing from one hour to another what is to become of us, or where we are to lay our heads. Indeed, our tribulations have been incredible, and almost unbearable. For more than four months we have been unable to say Mass, having no vestments or altar, and no cabin where we can be quiet or in safety for half an hour. Hardly any of our native priests can say Mass either; and what is worse, the sick die without receiving the last Sacraments. Everything is destroyed or burnt; all are scattered, everyone is in hiding. Hardly a person knows where I am, for I have no one to whom I can entrust a letter; and the communications from others to me are lost, as the people, afraid of being compromised, generally burn them. We are, in fact, reduced to the last extremity."

This sad letter was written in October, 1858. In December Fr. Vénard continued the recital in a long letter to his young brother, which we will transcribe literally.

"MY DEAREST EUSEBIUS,—I received in October last your letters and those that all my dear family wrote to me in 1857 and 1858. You may fancy the joy they gave me. I wish I could, in reply, give you some consoling intelligence, but, alas! nothing but misery, tears, and agony has flooded this unhappy Annamite mission for the last nine months. I wrote you in May, 1858, that the mandarins of Nam-Dinh had vented their satanic rage against the Christians by inflicting unheard-of tortures, and that they had published a fresh edict against us, more bloody than any that had preceded it. At that time the district where Theurel and I lived was comparatively quiet; but the seizure by the mandarins of some letters which we had written to the Christians of Nam-Dinh, was the signal for the outburst of a more violent persecution than we had before experienced. The bearer of our letters was put to the torture, and in his agonies disclosed everything, betraying the sites of Bishop Retord's new colleges of Vinh-Tri, Kê-Non, and Hoàng-Nguyên. At the same time, the devil entered the heart of one of our disciples, who, like another Judas, revealed to the mandarins not only the interior organization of the diocese, but all our hiding-places and our means of escape from persecutors. Fr. Theurel and I, though very anxious, flattered ourselves that, by being perfectly quiet, we might remain where we were; but the spies were too well informed.

"On the 10th of June, in the middle of the night,

a Christian woke us hurriedly, to say that the troops
were marching to surround our house and make us
prisoners. It was necessary to pack our traps and
flee. This was no easy matter. We were two Europeans, three Annamite Fathers, ten or fifteen catechists, more than a hundred students, and we had all
the mission furniture besides, which was to be put
in some place of safety. But our Annamites are so
accustomed to these sudden flights, that in a couple
of hours everything was hidden in different corners.
On the morning of St. Barnabas' Day, the mandarin's troops arrived to the number of two thousand,
while upwards of fifteen hundred young pagans of
the neighborhood were told off to watch all avenues
to the college. In a few minutes they had surrounded
not only the college itself, but three villages, the inhabitants of which were nearly all Christians. They
thought themselves sure of their prey. Happily, we
had been warned in time, and had placed our poor
students in distant villages; there were only two who
had delayed their departure and these were caught in
the very act of escaping; they were instantly honored with a 'cangue.' The soldiers had been promised a rich plunder but found nothing, only bare walls
and houses which looked as if they had been abandoned
for ages. In their rage they scattered all over
the surrounding country, and came upon a village
where the greater part of our students had taken
refuge. These would certainly have been seized, if
they had not received an early intimation of their
danger. There were only about ten laggards, whom
the soldiers caught as they were fleeing across the
fields, and whom they tortured as they had the former
captives. Among these was an old deacon over seventy
years of age. The mandarins, being unable to discover

catechists, priests, or students in the first four villages,
carried off our poor old porter, a blind man whom
we employed to pick rice, and a poor old woman
(with her daughter) who had the care of the church.
The houses of the principal Christians were spared,
owing to the intervention of the colonel and the
sub-prefect, who were friendly towards us.

"Well, the mandarins returned in triumph with our
dear prisoners, all wearing the 'cangue' around their
necks as criminals, and exposed to the derision of
the unbelievers, even as Jesus was when He bore His
Cross towards Calvary. This seizure was followed
by the capture of several other Christians, among
whom were three Annamite priests. In all more than
fifty persons were taken. Our confessors had to
endure frightful torments and scourgings; but all
preferred death to apostasy. One of the mandarins
tried to make a young catechist trample the Cross.
The catechist replied, 'If you were told to trample
under foot a coin bearing the image or superscription
of the emperor, would you dare do it?' A great box
on the ear was the answer. Another, taking the
crucifix tenderly in his hand, and looking at it, said,
'Dear Lord! Thou hast never done anything but
good, and they wish me to insult Thee! How could I
have the heart?' Twenty strokes of the terrible 'rotin'
were the reward of this outburst of love and piety.
The mandarins ordered the students to chant their
usual prayers. They intoned at once the litany of
the Saints, and when they came to the petition for
the king and for the mandarins, they repeated three
times, with great fervor, 'Deliver them, O Lord, from
all evil!' The mandarins understood the reproach and
commanded them to hold their tongues. Then they
tried to compel the old woman and her daughter to

apostatize, but both refused, and the old woman
said, 'Who would be fool enough to walk on the
head of his father or mother?' The judges, ashamed
of being defeated by a simple old woman, sent her
back to her village with the child.

"As to the rest,—the three priests were beheaded;
the two catechists and the poor old deacon died under
torture; and the others were exiled to an unwhole-
some and wild mountainous district, where many
have preceded, and where many will follow them.
May our Lord support and strengthen them! They
are fools for Christ's sake. Yet theirs is the only
true wisdom. What they have sown here below in
suffering and humiliation, they will reap above in
glory and in joy.

"Our churches, colleges, and houses have been
burnt to the ground. And this is not all. The Christians have been exposed to the most unjust and rapacious extortions. How can I describe to you what
leeches these Annamite officials are, from the highest
to the lowest? The first thing a mandarin does when
he visits a province is to ask if the 'king's orders have
been executed.' In other words, he says, 'Bring me
some money.' When he leaves it is the same thing.
The underlings are worse. They quarter themselves
upon the Christians, and if these do not at once give
all they ask, they denounce them to the authorities,
who throw them in prison. The people give them
the nickname, 'mandarin horse-flies.' What makes
these officials more vexing is the continual movement
among them, each one looking upon his province as
a place from which he must suck as much blood as
possible in a short time. I have neither the time nor
the heart to relate to you the turpitudes and villainies
of these people, and that not to the Christians only,
but to all who may be under their rule.

"The fate of our college of Hoàng-Nguyên has been equally that of Kê-Non and Vinh-Tri, but the last has suffered most. I cannot tell you all the details, as our communications have been interrupted, and patrols placed on all the roads to prevent the Christians from meeting, or to compel them to trample the Cross under foot. But I know that out of nine hundred souls, thirty or forty of the principal people have been thrown into prison and most horribly tortured; yet they have stood firm, and a large number have been condemned to death.

"It is not only Bishop Retord's diocese that has suffered so terribly. The persecution has swept over the whole country from Cambogia to China. The Spanish Dominicans have been even more cruelly treated than ourselves. The order has come to seize all Christians, and to put them to death by what is called 'lang-tri,' that is, slow torture, cutting off first the ankles, then the knees, the fingers, the elbows, and so on till the victim is nothing but a mutilated trunk. Bishop Melchior, the Dominican Vicar Apostolic of the eastern district of Tong-king, suffered this horrible death last August. But you will ask me, 'How did *you* manage to escape the fury of a storm like this?' I can only reply, 'By the grace of God, who has me in His holy keeping, and considers that my hour has not yet come. Our Christians guard my cabin and the only thing for me to do is to keep myself in a little corner without speaking or making the least noise. Even a sneeze or a cough might betray me. We consider ourselves fortunate if, in these retreats, we can have a little hole for light, so as to be able to read our office and some comforting book. In this weary but voluntary imprisonment one has to learn patience, and give up one's life freely to Divine Providence. Then, if the mandarin seems inclined to search the house, we take advantage of the darkness to escape to another hiding-place. Sometimes in a temporary lull, or a favorable moment, we are able to get a little fresh air, and to stretch our cramped limbs.

"The great misery of this state of things is that we cannot administer the Sacraments, and many of our converts have to die without any spiritual consolation. Another misfortune is that we nearly always compromise the Christians who give us hospitality, so that we often prefer trusting ourselves to the loyalty and good faith of pagans, who are less suspected. Fr. Theurel and I stayed two days and two nights in one of these houses; but we did not meet its owner, who hid himself, that he might not see a European face. One night we received a sudden notice to leave this asylum and only a quarter of an hour afterwards the troops of the mandarins arrived. Bishop Retord, seeing the way in which we were hunted, advised us to take refuge, as he and Bishop Jeantet had done, in the mountain. We went, but the apostate before mentioned got an inkling of this, and surrounding the cavern where the Bishops had lately been concealed, placed guards at all the mountain passes. But God watched over His servants and they escaped to the forests before the enemy had completed preparations. The mandarins searched all the caves, and carried off everything they could find, which, in fact, was all that we possessed; but no one was taken prisoner.

"Bishop Retord, Fr. Charbonnier, and Fr. Mathevon wandered barefoot through the woods, half dead with hunger, their feet wounded at every step by the pointed stones which the Annamites call *cats' ears,* and with no means of quenching their thirst but a villainous kind of water which no one can drink with impunity. Seeing no way of escape, they built themselves a little cabin in the centre of the forest, and remained there four months, during which time they were fed by neighboring Christians, and preserved in spite of the danger of being devoured by bears and tigers. I sent one of my catechists to them in August, and he was met by a magnificent royal tiger which had that very day eaten two poor girls who had been pasturing their bullocks on the roadside. My poor catechist was saved only by a miracle from a like fate. Dear brother, you will want to know if Bishop Retord is still in his forest home. His body, yes; but his spirit has left this vale of misery for a better world. A malignant fever carried him off on the 22nd of October. Thus ended his life of labor and suffering, after twenty-five years spent on the missions, and fifteen in the episcopate. He did not live to see peace dawn on this unhappy country. All his days had been passed amid persecutions and contradictions, the realization of a dream which he had as a child, when the Virgin appearing carried him to the top of a high mountain, to the foot of a great Cross, and told him his life would be a series of crucifixions to the end. All missioners have to follow the way of the Cross, but Bishop Retord did so more than any of us, and his death in this terrible forest, where he was exposed to the continual attacks of wild beasts, and had not even the commonest necessities of life, was indeed death on the Cross—naked, austere, like that of his Lord and Master.

"When Bishop Retord died he was alone with Fr. Mathevon, for as Fr. Charbonnier had had a touch of the fever, the Bishop had sent him down to the plains

to be nursed in the house of a pious Christian. After
our holy Bishop had expired, Fr. Mathevon took
shelter in a less unhealthful place, where he remains
concealed. As for Fr. Theurel, Fr. Titaud, and myself, we too had to climb the mountains, walk with
bleeding feet on the *cats' ears* and install ourselves as
hermits in the forest. We remained a fortnight in
perfect peace, and each day added some improvement
to our Robinson Crusoe life. We collected rain-
water to drink, and to use in cooking our provisions;
then we made a little straight avenue where we could
walk and recite our office. Every morning the inhabitants of the village of Dông-Chiem brought us
provisions; and we had just begun to dig the ground
and plant some vegetables, when one morning we had
an unexpected visit from six pagans, armed to the
teeth, who came in the guise of tiger-hunters. We
received them with great civility, and a few moments
after, under pretense of going out into the adjoining
forest to get some wood, we escaped rapidly down
the mountain-side to a boat which we kept on the
river always ready for emergencies. These 'hunters'
were in reality spies sent by the mandarins. From
that moment we resolved to live in our boat among
the reeds, now in one place, now in another. A
faithful and devoted young Christian came every
day, on the pretext of going fishing, to bring us food.
Our life as sea-birds went on for some weeks, when
we found that we were again discovered and watched.
So we were compelled to separate, and to seek shelter
in different houses. I returned to my old district and
lived for three weeks in the house of a catechist, but
amid continual alarms. I then took lodgings at Bût-
Dông, in a convent, where I still remain. This village is half Christian, half pagan; and in case of alarm

TOMB OF TU DUC,

Emperor of Annam, who condemned Theophane Vénard to death.

I have promised not to leave it, but to hide in a
cavern which has been prepared for me. Fr. Saiget,
who had been imprisoned for three months in a dark
place, escaped through a hole in the roof, and has
been able to come and join me. Just now we are
enjoying a certain tranquillity. The nuns have given
up their own room, which is large enough for us
to walk six or seven steps, and two of our catechists
are with us. So we study Chinese together to occupy
time. But the spies of the mandarins surround us,
and the poor nuns are in continual terror. There are
sixteen of them and they take turns watching day
and night. On the other hand, it is an immense
consolation for them to have the Sacraments, and we
strive to console and strengthen them to the utmost
of our power.

"We are in daily expectation of peace. A French
squadron arrived at Touranne on the 1st of September, and three thousand soldiers are camped on
the shore. As soon as their arrival was known, there
was great rejoicing among pagans as well as Christians, for the pagans hate the reigning dynasty and
attribute all the misfortunes of late years to the bad
conduct of the king, who thinks of nothing but
pleasure, and neglecting his people, gives them up to
the oppression and rapacity of mandarins. Many say,
'The cruelties against the Christians have brought
down the vengeance of the gods on this dynasty. The
Europeans come to deliver them, which is just and
fair.' The appearance of a comet has strengthened
the popular belief in the approaching dissolution of
the Government. Such phenomena are always a sign
of war to a superstitious people. A revolt has been
organized, and waits only for the reported success of
the French troops to lift its standard from one end

of the country to the other. Strangely enough, although the French squadron has been for three months and a half in Cochin-China, we have heard nothing."

CHAPTER XIII.

In the Caves.

"I have just heard that six more of our Christians have won the martyr's palm. Four were priests. One of our young students—of a noble family—who had had the misfortune to apostatize under torture, overwhelmed with remorse, gave himself up again into the hands of the cruel mandarin of Nam Dinh, who, in his fury, had him crushed to death under elephants' feet. Bishop Jeantet says he was quite a little fellow, and in one of the youngest classes. He adds, 'Our older students were superhuman in faith and fortitude. One of them, covered with blood, said, smiling, to the torturers, 'Your pincers and scourges are nothing to us; try something else!'

"Fr. Legrand de la Lyraie, one of our missioners in the eastern district, writes for Admiral Rigault de Genouilly, who commands the French squadron in the Chinese waters, imploring us to seek refuge on board his French steamer until the necessary measures are taken by the French army to deliver the Annamite Christians from oppression. The admiral is excessively alarmed at the dangers with which we are threatened, and wishes to put our lives out of the reach of the persecutors. Unfortunately, his proposal is impossible to us poor missioners of the western district; we are too far from the sea, and journeying in the country is too perilous to be attempted. I have

11

answered Fr. Legrand's kind letter and enclose this one in his, although there is fear that they will not reach their destination. I pray the Holy Angels to guard and conduct in peace the two devoted women who will be the bearers of my epistles! Women are our letter-carriers everywhere and manage it much better and with greater facility than men. Adieu."

This letter was dated December 21, 1858, and reached its destination in March, 1859, God having watched over the faithful messengers, so that they reached the French squadron at Touranne in safety. In July, 1859, similar letters were despatched by our missioner, but they were intercepted and never touched the soil of France. It was not till March, 1860, that Theophane again put pen to paper. But already his father had gone to announce in Heaven the coming of his son. His three children, grouped around the bed, had implored his benediction, and Mélanie, faithful to her promise, held before her father's dying eyes the portrait of his absent one. "Dearest father, Theophane is also here; you must bless him with us." The poor father gave a deep sigh, and murmured faintly, "Ah, that dear child! where is he?" . . . Then, gathering all his strength, and raising himself in his bed, he exclaimed, "Dear children, receive this, the last blessing of your father, in the name of the Father, and of the Son, and of the Holy Ghost. Amen." His uplifted hand fell heavily back on the bed. Then he looked upwards with a fixed expression for some minutes, and those around him felt that he must have seen a beautiful vision. So this good man fell asleep sweetly in God, and his pure, honest soul passed without struggle to its rest. The death occurred at noon on Friday, the 26th of August,

1859, M. Vénard being sixty-four years of age. His children had the following inscription engraved on his tomb:—

"Lord! He shared in Thy sacrifice; grant that he may share in Thy peace."

The sad news was at once conveyed to Tong-king but the unhappy state of that country prevented the arrival of the letters; and Theophane never knew on earth of his father's death.

But let us return to the Mission. After Bishop Retord's death, Bishop Jeantet—who was about seventy years of age—remained alone to administer the vast diocese. He chose Fr. Theurel to act as his coadjutor; and this devoted missioner, a bosom friend of Theophane, was consecrated Bishop of Acanthus, though only twenty-nine years old. If God had given peace for a short time to the persecuted Church, much might have been done by these two men, the one of such ripe wisdom and experience, the other with such fervent zeal and burning love of souls. But our Lord permitted the still further desolation of this land; and the following letter from Fr. Vénard gives an account of the first and last persecution of which he was to be the witness and the *victim*. The letter is addressed to an old college friend, the Abbé Paziot, and is dated the 10th of May, 1860.

"MY DEAR FRIEND,—It is a long time since I have written to you and perhaps you may fancy that I am dead, or that time has swept away our old friendship. Now I hope that both suppositions will disappear when you see this monstrous bit of paper—the only

thing I can get—on which I shall try to paint for you
—I have nothing but a brush—a description of our life
here, in as good language as a poor missioner can
command who has nearly forgotten his native tongue.

"I write to you from Tong-king, and from a little
dark hole, where the only light comes through the
crack of a partially opened door, just making it
possible for me to trace these lines, and now and
then to read a few pages of a book. For one must
be ever on the watch. If the dog barks, or a stranger
passes, the door is instantly closed, and I prepare
to hide myself in a still lower hole, which has been
excavated in my temporary retreat. This is the way
I have lived for three months, sometimes alone, sometimes in company with my dear old friend, Bishop
Theurel, now coadjutor to our Vicar Apostolic. The
convent which formerly sheltered us has been
destroyed by the pagans, who got wind of our being
there. We had barely time to escape into a space
about a foot wide between two double walls. We
could see through the chinks the band of persecutors,
with the mayor at their head, garotting five or six
of the oldest nuns, who had been left behind when
the younger ones took flight. They beat these poor
women with rods, laying their hands on everything
they could get, even a few earthenware pots which
hung on the partition behind which we were concealed. And we heard them vociferating, howling
like demons, threatening to kill and burn everybody
and everything unless they were given a large sum
of money. Their 'agreeable visit' lasted four hours;
and we were so close that we almost touched them.
We did not dare to make the smallest movement, and
held our breath till our pursuers were invited by the
principal people of the village to go out and eat and

get drunk with them. They did not go, however, without leaving guards to surround the house; so it was not till cock-crow in the morning that we could make our escape, and take refuge in a smoky dung-heap belonging to a pious old Christian widow, where we were joined by another missioner who had had equal difficulties in making good his retreat.

"What do you think of our position, dear old friend?—three missioners, one of whom is a bishop, lying side by side, day and night, in a space about a yard and a half square. Our only light comes through three holes the size of a little finger, made in the mud wall, and these a poor old woman is obliged to conceal by some fagots thrown down outside. Under our feet is a brick cellar, constructed with great skill by one of our catechists; in this cellar are three bamboo tubes, cleverly contrived to have their openings to the fresh air on the borders of a neighboring lake. This same catechist has built two other similar hiding-places in this village with several double partition walls.

"We stayed with our poor old widow three weeks, during which time I am afraid you would have been rather scandalized at our gaiety. When the three holes gave no more light, we had a little lamp, with a shade to prevent its tiny rays from penetrating outside through the chinks of our prison. One day we found ourselves surrounded, in fact completely blocked, by sentinels posted at every corner of the house, so that there was no possibility of passing from one house to the other. An apostate who knew that we were in the village, had betrayed our hiding-place. Well, God defeated his plans. From morning till night, the pagans passed and repassed us, upset everything in the house, searched every corner. They broke in the walls behind which we were concealed, and I thought our hour of martyrdom had come. But vain are the efforts of men when God opposes their designs! Perhaps you will say, 'In such a place, without air, light, or exercise, how can you live?' Your question is perfectly reasonable; and, what is more, you might ask why we don't go mad. To be shut up between two walls, with a roof which one can touch with his hand; having for our companions, —spiders, rats, and toads; obliged always to speak in a low voice, 'like the wind,' as the Annamites say; receiving every day terrible news of the torture and death of our fellow-missioners, of the destruction of missions, the exile of our students, and occasionally, worse still, of their apostasy under torture,—to live thus and not be utterly discouraged and cast down, we require, I admit, a special grace, a grace fitted to our state, I suppose.

"As to our health, we are like poor plants in a cellar, stretching our lanky, unhealthy branches toward the light and air. When I can put my mouth close to the door which guards our retreat, I own occasionally to a feeling of envy for those who can enjoy as much of God's fresh air and sunshine as they please. One of my brethren writes to-day that for eighteen months he has not seen the sun, and he dates his letter 'from the land of moles.' As for me, I live on without being too bilious; the weak points about me are the nerves. I want something strengthening, like wine, but we have barely enough to say Mass, so one must not think of it. I have some pills now which an Annamite doctor has made up for me instead. Not many days ago, I managed to pass into a neighboring house, and was very much astonished to find myself tottering like a drunken man. I had

lost the habit and almost the power of walking, and
the daylight made me giddy.

"I wrote to my family in 1858, to tell them of the
French squadron at Touranne. In 1859 the troops
destroyed the fortifications of Saigon, in Cochin-China,
leaving a garrison in one of the forts of the river.
Then in the summer came news of the war with
Austria, and a pestilential sickness which began to
decimate the French forces. Nevertheless, hostilities
were resumed against the Annamites in the autumn
and continued till April, 1860, when, to the astonishment of everyone, the French retreated, and abandoned
all the points which they had previously occupied."

Then follows a long comment on this retirement of
the French troops, ending with, " 'Man proposes, and
God disposes.' An expedition undertaken by the iron
will of the Emperor Napoleon III., and confided to
such a man as Admiral Rigault de Genouilly, ought
to have been crowned with success. But what are
human probabilities to the Divine decrees? God has
permitted that our deliverance should be delayed, and
our Church still further purified by suffering."

"The Annamite government, seeing the French
leave their shores, determined once for all to extir-
pate the Catholic faith throughout the kingdom.
Mandarins in any way favorable to the Catholics
were dismissed, and replaced by others whose hatred
was well known. Crosses were placed at the entrance
to all villages that the Christians might be forced to
trample them. Horribly blasphemous verses were
chanted, declaring that *Zato,* the Annamite name of
'Jesus,' had a dog for his father; and men were found
vile enough to carve crucifixes with a figure of a dog
on one side and a woman on the other, so as to de-
grade to the utmost the God of the Christians." He

alludes to other blasphemies even worse, and continues, "The government has established in each canton
a new functionary, who is called 'the shepherd of
the flock' (you may imagine he should rather be
called the 'wolf'), and in each mayoralty an officer
styled 'the strong man of the village.' Both these
men are employed in hunting down the unhappy
'Zato,' or followers of Christ, who, being beyond the
pale of law and justice, are exposed to every species
of ignominy, suffering, and wrong, without hope of
redress. Then there is a curious law in this country
which makes a whole village suffer for the offense of
one member. Therefore if a priest is found in a
place, especially a European, the town is razed to the
ground, half the inhabitants put to death, the rest
scattered to the four winds, while the mayor or chief
functionaries will be exiled and degraded if they have
concealed the white man, or will receive a large sum of
money if they have betrayed him. Who could resist
such a temptation?

"Again, on account of the destruction of our college, more than twelve hundred young men are
without home or occupation, not daring to return to
their families (if they have any), and wandering from
one Christian mission to another till they almost
inevitably fall into the hands of the persecutors.
Scarcely one of these has yielded to the cruelty or
blandishments of his tormentors, and the Church
may indeed be proud of having engendered such noble
confessors of the faith. But you see, dear friend,
how impossible it is for us, pastors of the flock, to
console our poor, suffering children or break the
bread of life for them. We are compelled to hide
ourselves and leave our lambs to the wolves. And
then in this country the more insolent the nobles

are, the more cowardly are the people, who become practically slaves. The women, too, are treated as children without souls; and although they are models of chastity and of zeal for the faith, they are so frightened that they almost lose their senses. It is only the nuns, who have had a longer and more careful Christian training, who can calmly brave the persecutors. When the French squadron appeared in 1859, the officials here persuaded themselves that the missioners had sent for it and that we were in league with the rebels to upset the reigning dynasty and to help on the revolution. They therefore seized the principal Christians in each village and threw them into prison, a terrible blow to the poor of the congregation, who had no longer any protectors whatever against their cruel oppressors. Out of seventy Annamite priests in this district, ten have already earned the martyr's palm; seven others are waiting in prison for the moment when death shall put an end to their torments. More than a thousand priests and laymen are exiled in the mountains.

"I began this letter in a little hiding-place in the midst of a fervent Christian population. In vain the mandarin, who has the hatred of a demon against Christ, has employed every possible agent to destroy or weaken their faith. He has failed because the whole population is of one mind and he cannot put all the people to death. To revenge himself he sends bands of young pagans to announce his arrival, to seize and gag the young girls, and to commit every species of atrocity. When he does not come, they are released only on payment of immense sums. So our Christians are always on the *qui vive;* to escape these horrors, men, women, and children flee to the rice-fields, and remain night and day concealed in mud and water. Sometimes the poor girls have been brought back to us half dead with the cold from this kind of exposure. One day the mandarin announced his visit, and his satellites were carrying on their work of pillage and brutality in every house. Suddenly they discovered one of our hiding-places, which, happily, was empty. They made a great fuss about this, and next morning, sent masons, with spades and hoes, to dig in every Christian house until they could find us. But Providence watched over us and we made our escape. I am now in the midst of pagans, not knowing what is going to happen next. They appear kind and benevolent; but God alone can read to the bottom of their hearts. They have a high idea of hospitality, and would hardly wrong a stranger who has come so far to seek it. Perhaps God has chosen such protectors so that the light of Gospel truth may shine upon them. Dear old friend! as I write this, the thought of all our misfortunes nearly overwhelms me, and I can hardly restrain my tears. Before this terrible persecution our mission was so flourishing! so many souls were being harvested! And now I feel like Jeremiah groaning over the ruins of Jerusalem. Will these ruins ever be rebuilt? It is like Ezekiel's vision of the dry bones. Can they ever be resuscitated? I have given you a summary of our misfortunes, but they are aggravated by a multitude of little circumstances which I should only weary you by enumerating. *'Magna est velut mare contritio tua!'*†

"But as for myself, dearest friend, I have confidence in God that I shall accomplish my course, preserving

---

†Great as the ocean is thy sorrow.

intact the deposit of Faith, Hope, and Charity; and that finally, by the merits of our Lord, I shall share with His friends the crown of the just. I wrote to my father in June, 1859, but I fear the letter has never reached him. Send him this one, and let him feel it is as if written to himself; and ask him to redouble his prayers for his poor little child-missioner. Dear father! he must be getting old now! I cannot help being anxious for tidings of him and all; for two years I have heard nothing.

"Dearest Mélanie,—I meant to have written a separate letter to you, as also to my brothers; but this one must do for you all. I have had no news of you since December, 1858; but I do not doubt that you have written, and perhaps a few months hence I may get your letters. Adieu! and God bless you, my much-loved ones. May you become greater saints day by day.—Your own devoted

Theophane."

"I commend myself especially to your prayers."

The contents of this letter, and especially its conclusion, point to the sad but glorious end which was at hand. The missioners, hunted like wild beasts, could no longer find a place of shelter; it is inconceivable how they could have endured their trials and misfortunes so long. In the meantime, Fr. Titaud, exhausted by the underground life which he had been compelled to lead for two years, expired on the 29th of January, 1860. Fr. Néron, betrayed into the hands of the enemy, underwent the torture of the knout, and was thrown into prison, where he remained for three months, of which twenty-one days were spent without any other nourishment than a few drops of water in the morning. At last he was beheaded, and thus fulfilled a curious prophecy which had been made concerning him at Paris in 1848.

"Fr. Néron has left us," writes Bishop Theurel, "and has passed from the battle-field to the rank of martyr; Fr. Vénard is taking the same road and will soon be with him in Heaven." The heroic close of this young apostle's life must form the subject of another chapter.

CHAPTER XIV.

Arrest and Martyrdom.

THE letter contained in the preceding chapter was written in May, 1860. Of the events that followed, Bishop Theurel says,—

"Fr. Vénard was living in a pagan village, preaching and teaching with great success, although the people said that, to declare themselves Christians, they must wait till the persecution had ceased a little. But when the chief of the province intimated that he considered him as his prisoner, Fr. Vénard went on to the Christian village of Kê-Bêo. He found superstitions of all kinds rampant in this place, and remained, desiring, as he said, 'a hand-to-hand fight with the devil.' God crowned his labors with wonderful success; after a few months the whole character of the place was changed, and a fervent Christian population replaced the timid, superstitious flock which he had found on his arrival. After this, he spent twenty days in the village of Kêm-Bâng, strengthening and consoling the terrified Christians, and incessantly teaching and administering the Sacraments. He went on then to Bût-Sôn, one of our noted missions in this terrible thirty years' persecution. In this village he found a devout native priest, and with him worked wonders among the people. Bishop Jeantet joined him here; and a few days after, Fr. Vénard, leaving the venerable bishop in safety in this almost impreg-

nable fortress, went back to Kê-Bêo. The good
effects of his previous visit were still apparent, and
Fr. Vénard thought that he might remain in peace,
to complete the good work. But he promised his
catechist, Luông, that he would return very shortly
to the safer refuge of Bût-Dông, as everyone was
extremely anxious about his safety. These were
indeed critical days.

"On the 30th of November, about nine o'clock in
the morning, five or six junks, carrying about twenty
men, appeared a few yards from the missioner's
house. As it was an isolated building, and the floods
covered the whole country, these junks were able to
guard every avenue. They were led by an old chief
of a neighboring hamlet, named Cai-Dô, the same
who in 1854 had contrived the escape of Fr. Néron
from the custom-house, but who now came on a
totally different errand. Leaving his junks, he
marched with five or six of his men to the mission
house. Fr. Vénard, instantly realizing the whole plot,
had retired between the usual double walls. The
chief, arriving at the house, cried out, 'Let the
European priest come forth.' At these words, the
catechist, Khang, who was busy hiding Fr. Vénard's
property, came forward boldly, and said, 'It is I
who inhabit this house, although I have only lately
arrived. If you will leave me in peace I shall be
thankful; but if not, I shall be resigned.' The chief,
making a signal to his men to garotte the catechist,
marched straight into the house, and giving a great
kick to the thin double partition which concealed the
missioner, seized Fr. Vénard, and dragged him
brutally to the junks, with his servant. It was a very
fine capture accomplished with no risk whatever. By
the time the faithful villagers of Kê-Bêo heard a

rumor of the event, the junks were well out of sight with their prey, and rescue was impossible. You may wish to know, dear Eusebius, who was the Judas that betrayed our dearest brother and Christ's chosen minister. There are different reports, but the most probable is that which fixes the treachery on Sû-Dôi, a pagan, related to the widow with whom the missioner lodged.

"The chief, having carried off the prisoners safely to his own home, made a great feast of rejoicing, after which he drove our dear missioner into a cage of bamboo, and put a 'cangue' on the neck of the catechist. Thus he took them to the prefecture. He stated that, when patrolling with his junks, he had come on these two men *outside* the jurisdiction of Kê-Bêo, and had hastened to bring them before the mandarin. He said this because he looked for a large reward, and also because the chief of Kê-Bêo was his own son-in-law, who would either share the booty or lose his place. But his *ruse* did not answer, for every one knew that the missioner was seized at Kê-Bêo; and as a consequence that village was heavily fined and had to pay more than eight hundred bars of silver, of which our poor community bore half. From his cage, Fr. Vénard penned the following letter, which I enclose with this one:

"'*December* 3, 1860.

"'My dearest People,—God in His mercy has permitted me to fall into the hands of the wicked. On the Feast of St. Andrew I was put in a square cage and carried to the prefecture, whence I trace these few lines for you, with some difficulty, by the aid of a paint-brush. To-morrow, December 4th, I am to appear before the judge. God knows what awaits me, but I do not fear. The grace of the Most High will be with me, and my Mother Mary will protect her poor little servant. I hope I shall be allowed writing materials; but I profit by this occasion, which a good pagan has given me, to send you love from my prison. The people of the household of the sub-prefect are full of kindness and attentions toward me, so I suffer very little. They come and visit me continually and allow me to speak freely. I take advantage of the opportunity to instruct them in the Christian faith. Many have owned to me their entire belief in our Creed, and say that the religion of Jesus Christ is the only one conformable to reason, and that if it were not for fear of the king and his terrible edicts they would gladly become Christians.

" 'Well, here I am in the arena of the Confessors for the Faith. Certainly God chooses the poor and weak things of this world to confound the mighty! I have confidence that the news of my fight will be equally that of my victory, for I do not lean on my own strength, but on the strength of Him who has overcome the powers of death and hell. I think of you all, my dearest father, my beloved sister, and brothers; and if I obtain the grace of martyrdom, oh, then still more shall I have you in remembrance! Adieu, my best loved ones, till our meeting in Heaven! In a moment I shall be adorned with the confessor's chains. Once more, adieu!' "

"The mandarin," wrote Bishop Theurel at this trying time, "was far from pleased at the arrival of the prisoners. Like Pilate, he protested loudly against taking innocent blood, and declared that the sin and the odium would fall on the heads of the captors, that for himself he kept the prisoners only because he did not dare to let them go. He was most civil to Fr.

Vénard, and changed his bamboo cage for a far more comfortable one of wood, higher and wider, so that the prisoner could put himself in any position he pleased. He also had a very light chain made for him, weighing only two pounds and a half; and this valued chain is now in my possession; our dear prisoner wore no other till his death. The prefect carried his condescension to the length of asking the missioner to dine in the audience chamber like a free man. After this a detachment of fifty or a hundred soldiers arrived to escort the prisoners to the capital, and the prefect sent with them a long letter explaining the circumstances of their arrest by the chief Dô, who formed part of the convoy."

Arrived at the capital, Fr. Vénard found means to write again to his family. We give this letter in full:

"January 2, 1861.

"MY DEAREST FATHER, SISTER, AND BROTHERS,—I write to you at the beginning of this year, which will be my last on earth. I hope you got the little note which I wrote announcing my capture on the Feast of St. Andrew. God permitted me to be betrayed by a traitor, but I owe him no grudge. From that village I sent you a few lines of farewell before I had the criminal's chain fastened on my feet and neck. I have kissed that chain, a true link which binds me to Jesus and Mary, and which I would not exchange for its weight in gold. The mandarin had the kindness to have a light one made for me, and treated me, during my stay in his prefecture, with every possible consideration. His brother came at least ten times and tried to persuade me to trample the Cross under foot. He did not want to see me die so young!

12

When I left the prefecture to go on to the capital, an immense crowd came to witness my departure; in spite of the guards and the mandarins, one man, a young Christian, was not afraid to throw himself on his knees three times before my cage, imploring my blessing, and declaring me to be a messenger sent from Heaven. He was of course made prisoner.

"After a couple of days I arrived at Kêcho, the ancient capital of the kings of Tong-king. Can you fancy me sitting quietly in the centre of my wooden cage, borne by eight soldiers, in the midst of an innumerable crowd of people, who almost barred the passage of the troops. I heard some of them saying, 'What a pretty boy that European is!' 'He is gay and bright, as if he were going to a feast!' 'He doesn't look a bit afraid!' 'Certainly he can't have done anything wrong!' 'He came to our country to do us good and yet they will put him to death!' etc., etc. We entered the citadel by the eastern gate and I was brought at once before the tribunal of the judge of criminal cases. My catechist Khang, bearing his terrible yoke, walked behind my cage. I prayed God's Holy Spirit to strengthen us both and to speak by our mouths according to our Savior's promise; and I invoked the Queen of Martyrs and begged her to help her faithful child.

"To begin with, the judge gave me a cup of tea, which I drank without ceremony in my cage. Then he commenced the usual interrogatory:

"'Whence do you come?' 'I am from the Great West, from the country of France.'

"'What have you come to do in Annam?' 'I have come to preach the true religion to those who know it not.'

" 'What is your age?' 'Thirty-one.' The judge here said aside, with an accent of pity, 'Poor fellow! he is still very young!' Then he continued, 'Who sent you here?' 'Neither the king nor the mandarins of France; but I myself, of my own accord, came to preach the Gospel to the heathen, and my superiors in religion assigned Annam to me as my district.'

" 'Do you know the bishop called, in the Annamite language, *Lieow?*' (Bishop Retord.) 'Yes, I know him.'

" 'Why did he give letters of recommendation to the rebel chiefs to enroll the Christians?'

"I ventured to ask the mandarin in reply, 'From what source did you derive that information?'

" 'The prefect of Nâm-Digne wrote us word of it.'

" 'Well, then, I can bear witness that it is not true. The Bishop was too wise to commit so foolish an act, and if letters were produced to prove it, I should know that they were false. I saw the circular which Bishop Lieow addressed to his priests, in which he positively forbade their joining the rebel chiefs and declared that he would a thousand times sooner sacrifice his life than dip his crozier in blood.'

" 'And the warriors of Europe, who took Touranne and Saigon,—who sent them? What was their object in making war on our country?'

" 'Mandarin—I heard the rumors of war; but having no communication with these European troops, I cannot answer your question.'

"At this part of the interrogatory the prefect arrived, and he had hardly taken his seat when he cried out to me, in a loud and angry voice,—

" 'Ah! you chief of the Christian religion, you have a clever countenance, you know very well that the Annamite laws forbid entrance into the kingdom to

Europeans; what was the use, then, of coming here to be killed? It is *you* who have excited the Europeans to make war upon us, is it not? Speak the truth, or I will put you to the torture.'

" 'Great mandarin, you ask me two questions. To the first I reply that I am sent as an ambassador from Heaven to preach the true religion to those who scorn it not, no matter in what kingdom, or in what place. We respect the authority of kings on the earth, but we respect more the authority of the King of Heaven. To your second question I answer that I never in any way invited or excited the Europeans to make war on the Annamite kingdom.'

" 'In that case will you tell them to go? And you will then obtain your pardon.'

" 'Great mandarin! I have no power and no authority in such matters, but if His Majesty sends me I will beg the European warriors to abstain from making war on the Annamites; and if I do not succeed, I will return here to suffer death.'

" 'You do not fear death, then?'

" 'Great mandarin! I do not fear death. I have come here to preach the true religion. I am guilty of no crime which deserves death. But if the Annamites kill me, I shall shed my blood with great joy for them.'

" 'Have you any spite or ill-will against the man who betrayed and took you prisoner?'

" 'None at all. The Christian religion forbids us to entertain anger, and teaches us to love those who hate us.'

" 'Chief of the Christian religion! You must declare the names of all the places and people that have sheltered you up to this hour.'

" 'Great mandarin! They call you the father and

mother of this people. If I were to make such a declaration it would involve a large number of persons in untold misery. Judge for yourself whether it would become me to do this or not.'

" 'Trample the Cross under foot, then, and you shall not be put to death.'

" 'How! I have preached the religion of the Cross all my life until this day, and do you expect me to abjure it now? I do not esteem so highly the pleasures of this life as to be willing to buy the preservation of it by apostasy.'

" 'If death has such a charm in your eyes, why did you hide yourself when there was fear of your being taken?'

" 'Great mandarin! Our religion forbids us to presume on our strength, and to deliver ourselves to the persecutors. But Heaven having permitted my arrest, I have confidence in God that He will give me sufficient courage to suffer all torture and be constant unto death.'

"This is a summary of the questions asked me, and of my answers. The mandarins then proceeded to question my catechist and inflicted ten strokes of the knout upon him. He bore them without flinching, God giving him strength all the while gloriously to confess the faith.

"Since that day I have been placed in my cage at the door of the prefect's house, guarded by a company of Cochin-Chinese soldiers. A great many persons of rank have come to visit me and converse with me. They will have it that I am a doctor, an astronomer, a diviner, a prophet, from whom nothing is hid. Several visitors have begged me to tell their fortunes. Then they question me about Europe, about France, in fact, about the whole world.

This gives me an opportunity to enlighten them a little on points about which they are supremely ignorant, and on which they have sometimes the most comical ideas. I try above everything to slip in a little serious word now and then so as to teach them the way of salvation. But the Annamites are a frivolous race, and don't like serious subjects; still less will they treat on philosophy or religion. On the other hand, their heart is good, and they do their best to show me both interest and sympathy. My soldier guards have an affection for me, and though they have been blamed two or three times for letting me go out, they still open my cage from time to time, and allow me to take a little walk. . . . Sometimes their conversation is not very proper, but I never let pass words of that sort; and I do not hesitate to speak to them strongly. I tell them that they lower themselves in the eyes of everyone by impure thoughts and libertine discourses; and that if they can talk in that way without blushing, they deserve nothing but pity, not to say contempt. My lessons make an impression. They are far more careful in their language now, and some have gone to the length of begging my pardon for having made use of indelicate expressions. Still I cannot say that everything is sweet and pleasant; although many are kind to me, some insult and mock me, and use rough language to me. May God forgive them!

"I am now only waiting patiently for the day when God will allow me to offer Him the sacrifice of my blood. I do not regret leaving this world; my soul thirsts for the waters of eternal life. My exile is over. I touch the soil of my real country; earth vanishes, Heaven opens, I go to God. Adieu, dearest father, sister, brothers, do not mourn for me, do

not weep for me, live the years that are yet left
to you on earth in unity and love. Practice your
religion; keep pure from all sin. We shall meet
again in Heaven, and shall enjoy true happiness in
the kingdom of God. Adieu. I should like to write
to each one separately but I cannot, and you know
my heart. It is three long, weary years since I have
heard from you, and I know not who is taken or
who is left. Adieu. The prisoner of Jesus Christ
salutes you. In a very short time the sacrifice will
be consummated. May God have you always in His
holy keeping. Amen."

Fr. Vénard's particular friend, Bishop Theurel, took
charge of this letter, and added, "The sentence of
our dearest Theophane has been pronounced. He is
to be beheaded, but the execution will probably be
delayed till the middle of February. In the meantime
he wants for nothing. And though in chains, he is
as gay in his cage as a little bird.

"As I was the nearest missioner to Kêcho, being
only one day's march from the capital, I was naturally
able to write to him three or four times. Bishop
Jeantet and Fr. Saiget wrote likewise; and our dear
prisoner was able to answer us pretty regularly. Our
medium of communication was a native Christian, the
head of the patrol, a man true as steel, named Huong-
Moï, whose house had been my refuge for two
months and who had mingled with the troop of servants at the prefecture, and obtained his present post
out of devotion to our sufferer. On the 28th of
December, Theophane wrote,—

" 'The mandarins wrote four days ago to announce
my capture to the king, but no answer has yet been

received. They made me sign a written declaration of
the circumstances of my arrest, countersigned by my
catechist Khang. I have taken care that it shall compromise no one. I am pretty well treated, and some
of the Cochin-Chinese soldiers are noble fellows. But
as I am kept at the door of the prefecture, I write
with difficulty. The great mandarin allows threepence a day for my food and I am in fairly good
health. My heart is as tranquil as a lake which re-
flects the blue sky and I have no fear. The mandarin
of Nam-Xang, who spends his life tormenting the
Christians, came to see me the other day, and I told
him that "Jesus was stronger than he; that it was in
vain he struggled with our Lord, and that he would
have to yield to His power in the end." The gaoler
Tû, who seized four priests in 1859, asked after you.
I told him publicly that "his was a vile trade; and
that his diploma as mandarin of the ninth class, the
price of treachery and blood, would fade as a wild-
flower in the Spring." At this the mandarin, judge,
and all the guards laughed and applauded. I think
they like and respect me, and the great mandarin has
twice invited me to dinner.'

"On the 3rd of January he wrote again: 'I have
received your loving letter. A thousand thanks! I
profit by the absence of the great mandarin to answer.
He used to allow threepence for my food, but now he
has stopped it. So I should have gone supperless to
bed to-day if the chief Maï, who is also in prison,
had not sent me a bowl of rice. The new mandarin
of justice came to see me yesterday and put me
through a fresh interrogation. When he said that
the happiness of the next world was doubtful, while
the joys of the present were certain and positive, I
replied, 'As for me, great mandarin, I find nothing

on earth which gives **real happiness**; riches create
envy and bring cares; sensual pleasures engender endless maladies. My heart is too large, and nothing
which you call happiness in this world satisfies it.'
On the whole, he was not uncivil. As he said that he
had given orders to have me well treated, I replied
that I had nothing to eat. He pretended not to understand me. So to-morrow the captain of the guard
says that he will go and renew the demand. In
spite of his fine speeches, this mandarin has doubled
my guard, and sends some one constantly to see if
my cage is closed. Among the gaolers is an excellent
fellow named Tièn, who shows me the most affectionate respect. He alone, with one of the captains, is
not afraid, in addressing me, to make use of the expression *"Bam lay"*—a term of reverence used only
to address mandarins or persons of high position.
On New Year's Day the captain of the guard brought
me a cup of first-class tea, and as the gaoler Tièn was
passing at the time, I invited him to share it with me,
which he did with a delicacy and a simplicity which
only the heart could teach, and which hypocrisy could
not counterfeit. But my letter runs on without a word
as to my feelings. I wrote a long letter to my family
on very bad paper, which I hope you received and will
kindly forward to them, filling up the details which
may be wanting. Ah! I am now come to the hour so
much desired by us all. It is no longer, as in the
"Hymn of Departure," *"Perhaps* some day," but
"Very soon all the blood in my veins

> Will be shed for Thee. My feet—oh, what joy!—
> *Are now* loaded with chains."

    " 'In the long, weary hours in my cage I think of

eternity. Time is, after all, so short when thus meas-
ured. You will repeat the words of St. Martin,
*"Domine, si adhuc populo tuo sum necessarius, non
recuso laborem,"*† while I can exclaim with St. Paul,
*"Jam delibor; et tempus resolutionis meae instat;
(tibi) vivere Christus est, mihi mori lucrum. O! quam
gloriosum est regnum in quo cum Christo gaudent
omnes sancti. . . . Audivi vocem . . . Beati mortui
. . . "*‡ These are words which, in spite of the persecution, we never failed to sing on All Saints' and
All Souls' Day, and which always touched us to
tears. I do not know if I shall ever be allowed to
write to you again. Good-bye! I should have been
very happy to have gone on working with you. I do
so love this Tong-king mission! But now, in place of
the sweat of my brow, I give it my blood. The
sword hangs over my head but I have no fears. Our
good God has taken pity on my weakness and filled
me with Himself so that I am happy, and even joyous. From time to time I astonish the mandarin's
household by singing,—

"O beloved Mother,
    Place me
  Soon in our true home
    Near Thee!
Noble Tong-king! land blessed by God!
  Thou glorious country of the heroes of faith!
I came to serve thee. I gladly die for thee.
  So be it, O Lord. Amen."

---

†O Lord, if I am still needful to Thy people, I will not refuse to labor.
‡I go now; the time of my dissolution is at hand. (For you) to live
is Christ; for me to die is gain. O, how glorious is the kingdom
in which all the saints rejoice with Christ. . . I heard a voice . . .
Blessed are the dead . . .

" 'When my head falls under the axe of the executioner, receive it, O loving Jesus! O Immaculate Mother! as the bunch of ripe grapes which falls under the scissors, as the full-blown rose which has been gathered in your honor. *Ave Maria!* I will say this also from you. *Ave Maria!'* (I had begged him with earnestness to salute Mary for me on his arrival in Paradise.)

" 'I should be very grateful if you could manage to send some remembrance of me to my family. My chalice was a family parting souvenir; if my brother Eusebius could have it, he would be in the seventh heaven of delight. . . . Oh, how glorious must be the kingdom in which the Saints rejoice with Jesus Christ our Lord! I heard a voice from Heaven saying, "Blessed are the dead that die in the Lord." '

"By this letter, written by your brother on the 3rd of January," continues Bishop Theurel, "you see that the mandarins had ceased to feed the prisoner of Jesus Christ. This was what we expected; so we directly employed a Christian widow, named Nghién, who happened to be a sister of the great mandarin's cook, to provide all that was necessary for him; and in that way we could have more frequent communications. On the 6th of January he wrote again:—

" 'I have just received your good wishes for the new year. Thanks! Yes; for once I have indeed a lucky chance. I ought to have sent you my affectionate wishes sooner but you will forgive the delay. A happy new year to my dear, reverend Bishop! Peace and labor, and then an eternal repose in the bosom of the Saviour! . . During the absence of the mandarin prefect, his wife, a young girl from Kêcho, recently married, came to pay me a visit; but when she saw me come out of my cage, she ran away like a child! I sent for her, and called her back as gently as I could; but when she did return she was so frightened that she could not open her mouth. Monseigneur, you must work at this—at the education of woman, to raise her from her present servile position, to establish schools for young girls, to teach them the beauty and grandeur of Christian womanhood. . . Let us say together once more, *"Tuus totus ego sum, et omnia mea tua sunt."* †

"Just at this time, in the prison of Kêcho, was an Annamite priest, named Khoân, who is there still. I was hoping that Theophane might be allowed to see him; but as their meeting seemed impossible, I sent the good Father Tinh, vicar of the parish of Kêcho, to comfort our dear prisoner. Huong Moï, that faithful head of the patrol whom I have before mentioned, undertook to introduce him into the mandarin's palace, and even to the cage of Fr. Vénard. The meeting took place on the 15th of January, in presence of the guards and of a whole crowd of people, the suite of the mandarins, who filled the hall. Your brother, pretending not to recognize Father Tinh, asked the chief of the patrol, 'Who is the gentleman that came in with you just now?' 'It is the *thay-ca,'* replied Huong Moï. (This expression signifies either a priest or the head of a family.) Poor Father Tinh felt his heart sink into his shoes at this word. But Huong Moï, who laughed at danger, made jokes with the people around, so as to hide the confusion of the priest and divert the people's attention. Fr. Vénard, being formally introduced as to a stranger, was let out of his cage, and allowed to walk in the garden, where he instantly made his confession,

---

† I am all Thine, and all that belongs to me is Thine.

none of the guards having followed him. When Fr.
Vénard came back to his cage, Huong Moï made a
fresh and a successful effort to amuse the assistants,
during which time Father Tinh approached the cage,
as if for the purpose of examining it, and said a few
words in a low voice to Fr. Vénard, giving him absolution. Then he walked quietly away. Your poor
brother gave them all some tea afterwards, and took
leave of Father Tinh. The latter had brought the
Blessed Sacrament, and left It with the devout widow
of whom I have spoken. She carried It to Fr. Vénard
in the evening, concealed in some bread. He therefore could enjoy the presence of our dear Lord till
midnight, after which he communicated. In a letter
to Bishop Jeantet, written on the 20th of January,
Theophane says with emotion,—

" 'Father Tinh will tell you of his visit, when I
gave him some tea in the midst of all the crowd. He
brought me, on the other hand, the Bread of the traveller,— *"Mi Jesus, Deus meus,"*† in my cage! Think
of that!' Then he goes on to say, 'I have not received a single stroke of the knout. I have had
very little insult, and much sympathy; no one here
wishes me to die. The people of the household of the
great mandarin are kindness itself to me. I have suffered nothing in comparison with my brethren. I
have only to lay my head quietly on the block, under
the axe of the executioner, and at once I shall find
myself in the presence of Our Lord, saying, "Here am
I, O Lord! Thy little martyr!" I shall present my

---

† My Jesus, my God.

palm to Our Lady, and say, "Hail, Mary! my Mother and my Mistress, all hail!" And I shall take my place in the ranks of the thousands killed for the holy name of Jesus; and I shall intone the eternal Hosanna! Amen.'

"I enclose the last letters, written to you all, which are of the same date as mine. It is impossible, I think, for any one to read them unmoved."

"J. M. J.†

"From my Cage, Kêcho,

"*January* 20, 1861.

"My dearest, much honored, and much loved Father,—As my sentence is still delayed, I will send you one more word of farewell, which will probably be the last. These last days in my prison pass quietly; all who surround me are civil and respectful and a good many love me. From the great mandarin down to the humblest private soldier, every one regrets that the laws of the country condemn me to death. I have not been put to the torture like my brethren. A slight sabre-cut will separate my head from my body, like the spring flower which the Master of the Garden gathers for His pleasure. We are all flowers planted on this earth, which God plucks in His own good time, some a little sooner, some a little later. One is as the blushing rose, another the virginal lily, a third the humble violet. Let us each strive to please Our Sovereign Lord and Master according to the gift and the sweetness which He has bestowed upon us. I wish you, my dearest father, a

---

†Jesus, Mary, Joseph.

long, happy, and peaceful old age, and that you may
bear the cross of life with Jesus unto the Calvary of
a happy death. Father and son, may we meet in
paradise. I, poor little moth, go first. Adieu!

      "Your devoted and dutiful son,

    "Theophane Vénard, Missionary Apostolic."

        "J. M. J.

    "FROM MY CAGE, IN TONG-KING,

          "January 20, 1861.

   "MY DEAREST SISTER,—I wrote, some days ago, a
general letter to the family, which I hope has reached
you, and in which I gave all the details of my capture
and interrogatory. Now, as my last hour is approaching, I want to send you, my darling sister and friend,
a special word of love and farewell. For our hearts
have been one from our childhood. You have never
had a secret from me, nor I from you. When, as a
school-boy, I used to leave home for college, it was
my little Mélanie who prepared my box, and softened
with her tender words the pain of parting. It was
you who shared in the sorrows and joys of my college life; it was you who strengthened my vocation
for the foreign missions. It was with you, dearest
Mélanie, that I passed that solemn night of the 26th
of February, 1851, which was our last meeting upon
earth, and which we spent in a conversation so full
of intimate thoughts and feelings of sympathy and
holy hope, that it reminded me of the farewell of St.
Benedict and St. Scholastica.

   "And when I crossed the seas, and came to water
with sweat and blood this Annamite country, your

letters were my strength, my joy, and my consolation. It is then only fair that, in this last hour, your
brother should think of you, and send to you a few
final words of love and never-dying remembrance.
. . . It is midnight. Around my wooden cage I see
nothing but banners and long sabres. In one corner
of the hall, where my cage is placed, a group of
soldiers are playing at cards; another group at
'*draughts.*' From time to time the sentries strike
the hours of night on their drums or 'tom-toms.'
About two feet from my cage, a feeble oil-lamp throws
a vacillating light on this sheet of Chinese paper and
enables me to trace these few lines.

"From day to day I expect my sentence. Perhaps
to-morrow I shall be led to execution. Happy death,
which conducts me to the portals of eternal life!
According to all human probability, I shall be beheaded,—a glorious shame, of which Heaven will be
the price! At this news, darling sister, you will shed
tears,—but they should be of joy! Think of your
brother, wearing the aureole of the martyrs, and
bearing in his hand the palm of victory! Only a few
short hours, and my soul will quit this earth, will
finish her exile, will have done with the fight. I
shall mount upwards and reach our own true home.
There, in that abode of God's elect, I shall see what
the eyes of man cannot imagine; hear harmonies
which his ear cannot dream of now; enjoy a happiness
which it has never entered into his heart even to
conceive!

"But before arriving at all this, the grain of wheat
must be ground,—the bunch of grapes must be trod-
den in the wine-press. May I become only pure bread
and wine, fit for the Master's use! I hope for this,
through the mercies of my Saviour and Redeemer,

" MÉLANIE,"
A Nun at Amiens.

through the protection of His Immaculate Mother.
So I venture, while still in the arena and in the midst
of the fight, to intone the hymn of triumph, as if I
were sure of victory. And you, my dearest sister, I
leave you in the field of virtues and good works.
Reap a great harvest of these for the eternal life
which awaits us both. Gather faith, hope, charity,
patience, gentleness, sweetness, perseverance, and a
holy death; and we shall be together, now and forevermore. Good-bye, my Mélanie! Good-bye, my
loved sister! Adieu! Your devoted brother,

J. T. Vénard, Missionary Apostolic."

"J. M. J.

"January 20, 1861.

"MY DEAREST HENRY,—I must send you also a few
lines of brotherly love and farewell. You were very
young when we parted, and a stranger to the world
and its pleasures. Ah! the heart of man is too large
to be satisfied with the deceptive and passing joys here
below, and I know you will not seek happiness where
it is not to be found. My dearest Henry, you are now
twenty-nine, the age of manhood. Be, then, a man.
Do not waste your life in the frivolities of the world.
To resist one's evil inclinations, to watch against the
snare of the Evil One, and to practise one's religion—
is to be really a man; not to do so, is to be less than
a man. I write these words to you at a solemn
moment. In a few hours—at most, in a few days—I
shall be put to death for the faith in Christ Jesus.
Yes, my own dear brother, I die with the conviction
that you will always love God, as you have loved
Him in your childhood. He is the God of your
fathers, the God of those who have given you life,
the God of your brothers and sister. He is the God

13

whom the greatest intellects humanity has ever known have served, worshipped and adored. He is the great and merciful God, the God who helps us to do right, and keeps us from evil—the God who alone will reward or punish us eternally.

"Read these words often; it is your best friend, your poor brother Theophane, who has written them. I leave to you the care of our dear father and sister. Be a good son and a good brother; a good Christian, in life and in death! Good-bye, dearest brother. Come and meet me in Heaven.

"One who loves you,

"Theophane Vénard, Missionary Apostolic."

"J. M. J.

"January 20, 1861.

"My much-loved one,—If I did not write you a few lines for your very own self, you would be jealous, and, I admit, with reason. You deserve it, too, for your many lengthy and interesting letters to me. It is very long since I have heard from you now; and perhaps you are already a priest? and—who knows?—perhaps a missioner? However that may be, by the time you receive this letter your brother will be no longer in this bad world, *totus in maligno positus*. He will have left it for a better one, where you must strive to rejoin him some day. Your brother's head will have fallen, and every drop of his blood will have been poured out for God. He will have died a martyr! That was the dream of my youth! When, as a little man nine years old, I took my pet goat to browse on the slopes of Bel-Air, I used to devour the life and the death of the Venerable Charles Cornay, and say to myself, 'And I, too, will go to Tong-king. And I, too, will be a martyr!' Oh, admirable thread of

Divine Providence, which has guided me through
the labyrinth of this life to the very mission of Tong-
king and to martyrdom! Bless and praise our good
and merciful God with me, dearest Eusebius, for
having taken such care of his miserable little servant.
Attraxit me, miserans mei!†

"Dear Eusebius, I have loved and still love these
Annamite people with an ardent affection. If God
had given me a long life, I would gladly have sacrificed every moment of it, body and soul, to the building up of the Church in Tong-king. The people are
so good, so fervent, so loyal! If my health, feeble
as a reed, did not enable me to do great things, at
least I had my heart in the work. But man proposes,
and God disposes: life and death are in His hand.
As for us, if He gives us life, let us live for Him;
if death, then let us die for Him.

"And for you, dearest little brother, still so young
in years, you will remain long after me, fighting
among the waves of this troublesome world. Guide
your ship well. Let prudence take the helm, humility
the rudder; let God be your compass, Mary your
anchor of hope. And then, in spite of the disgust
and bitterness which, like a howling sea, will sometimes overwhelm you, never be cast down. Have
confidence in God, and, like Noah's ark, swim always
above the waters. . . . . My lamp gives no more
light. Good-bye, my Eusebius, until the day when
you come to rejoin me in Heaven. Your most
affectionate brother,

"J. T. Vénard, Missionary Apostolic."

---

†Having mercy on me, He has drawn me to Himself.

These letters were accompanied by a note from Bishop Theurel, detailing the consummation of the sacrifice, as follows:—

"The 1st of February, Fr. Vénard wrote another little message, which reached me only after his martyrdom. He said,—

" 'The days of my pilgrimage lengthen strangely. The prefect is astonished that my sentence should be so long delayed. All the despatches from the king pass before my cage and each time one arrives I ask if my sentence of death is come. Each time the post-boy answers, 'No.' I hail every morning as the dawn of eternity, but evening comes, and I am still here. My reason and my heart announce to me daily the approach of death, but sometimes I have presentiments that the answer will not be death; I try to put this thought from me as a snare of the devil. Still the suspense is trying. Adieu, dear and loved Bishop. Will it be my last good-bye?—who knows? May the will of God be done, and not mine!'

"This farewell was really to be the last. During the night of February the 2nd the desired sentence arrived at last; but Fr. Vénard knew it not. At two o'clock in the morning he breakfasted as usual and was allowed to go into the garden. The widow Nghiên, having followed him stealthily, said in a low voice, 'Father, you are to be executed to-day.' And because your brother doubted, since he had been told that he was to be taken to the king, she added, 'It is quite certain. Already the elephants are ordered and the soldiers are ready; in a few moments you will be led to execution.' Fr. Vénard hastily returned to his cage to distribute his little effects among his friends. At this moment an old lady named Xin arrived,

bearing the Blessed Sacrament to the prisoner of
Jesus Christ. It was the fourth time that Father
Tinh had managed to convey to him the Bread of
Life. This pious lady, seeing that his moments were
counted, pressed through the crowd of soldiers to
the cage, and succeeded in putting into his hand the
tiny box which contained the Sacred Host. But it
was too bold a movement. No sooner had the poor
missioner received the treasure than the soldiers
threw themselves upon him, dragged the pyx from
him by main force, and gave it to their captain. Fr.
Vénard, forgetting everything in his terror lest the
Body of our Lord should be profaned, cried out to
the widow Nghiên, *They have taken away my Viaticum!* The courageous widow ran to the captain who
carried the box and told him that this mysterious
wafer was not, as he imagined, a poison to accelerate
death and to anticipate the ends of justice, but a food
for the passage from this life to another, and she
added, in a tone of conviction, 'If you venture to touch
this Viaticum, you and all your family will die
suddenly.'

"The captain, not knowing what to think of it all,
timidly gave back the box to the widow, who, on
account of the tumult, could not pass it to Fr. Vénard.
She returned the pyx therefore to Mdlle. Xin, who
sorrowfully, though safely, took it back to Father
Tinh.

"In the meantime, the mandarin had summoned the
missioner to hear his sentence and to be sent to execution. Fr. Vénard had prepared for himself a special
dress for this day of his nuptials, a garment of white
cotton covered with a long robe of black silk. Having
put it on, he calmly appeared before the mandarins,
and when the sentence of his death had been pro-

nounced, he took up his parable, and made a little
speech. This was a formal declaration that he had
come to Tong-king only to teach the true religion,
and that he was going to die for the same cause. He
ended by saying to the judges, *One day we shall
meet each other again, at the tribunal of God.* The
mandarin of justice rose hastily and exclaimed, 'I will
have no insolence!' The convoy was ordered to start
at once. It was composed of two elephants and two
hundred soldiers, commanded by a lieutenant colonel.
Fr. Vénard began to sing Latin psalms and hymns as
the procession passed through the town. The place of
execution was about half an hour from the mandarin's
house, and when they had arrived, the soldiers formed
a great circle to keep back the crowd, which was
enormous; but the courageous widow Nghièn broke
through the ranks and at last obtained permission to
remain with the missioner to the end.

"Fr. Vénard, with a calm and even joyous countenance, looked all over the crowd, hoping to see
Father Tinh, and to receive a last absolution. But
this poor priest, not knowing that the order for execution had been given, could not arrive in time. Your
brother, having given his sandals to the faithful
widow, sat quietly on his mat. The soldiers took off
his chain, and with a hammer loosened the nails
which fastened the ring about his neck and ankles.
Then they pushed all, even the poor widow, outside
the circle.

"The executioner was a hideous hunchback, called
Tûe, once a soldier, now a buffoon. He had already
decapitated four of our priests on the 25th of March,
1860, and had begged to be allowed to perform this
horrible office that he might have the martyr's clothes.
He began by asking of Fr. Vénard, as of an ordinary

criminal, what he would give him to be executed promptly and well. The answer he received was, *'The longer it lasts the better it will be!'* Seeing that the missioner's clothes were new and clean, his whole anxiety was to get them without any stains of blood. He therefore begged his victim to strip; and, as this first invitation remained unheeded, he added, with barbarous ingenuity, 'You are to be *lang-tri,*' that is, to have all the members cut off at the joints and the trunk sawn into four parts. Our dear missioner, either because he believed the lie, or because he wished to experience more fully the humiliation of our Saviour, who before His crucifixion bore similar treatment, perhaps also because he was anxious to get rid of the importunities of this vile hunchback, took off all his clothes except his trousers. His elbows were then tightly tied behind his back, forcing him to hold up his head for the fatal stroke, and he was fastened to a stake badly fixed in the ground. In this position, at a given signal, Fr. Vénard received the first stroke—but it was simply a trial blow on the part of the merciless executioner and did not enter the flesh deeply. The next stroke, more vigorously applied, cut the head nearly off, the stake and the victim falling together. Then the executioner, finding his sword blunt, took another, and hacked at the neck, while indignant murmurs rose from the crowd.

"Finally, seizing the fallen head by the ear, he held it up to the lieutenant colonel who presided at the torture. This officer, having desired the municipal authorities to keep watch for three days, during which time the head was to be exposed, instantly sounded the retreat and marched his troops back to their quarters. All this time the poor widow Nghiên and many other women were bewailing as if at the death of their first-born. No sooner had the troops left the ground than these women and a crowd of sympathizers precipitated themselves on the spot to soak their handkerchiefs and papers in the martyr's blood; and they showed such ardor that not a blade of grass was left in the place. The execution had not occurred in the usual spot. The great mandarin desired to have the missioner decapitated on the edge of the river, so that the head might be thrown into it with greater ease after the exposition. For this reason many of the curious, and likewise of the faithful, had taken the wrong road, among the rest a good pagan who had arranged for the burial of the body; hence, although the execution was at eight in the morning, at midday the body still remained extended on the sand, covered with a mat. Then, a bier having been brought down the stream, everything was prepared for the interment. Besides the family of this faithful pagan, named Huông-Da, the widow Nghiên, who had not left the remains for an instant, was present.

"The body was also guarded by a former Christian mayor, named Ly-Vûng, and a devout Catholic boatman from the southern district of Tong-king. The latter had the delicacy to wrap the martyr's body in his own coat, which he took off for that purpose. The whole was afterwards enclosed in a cotton sheet, tightly bound with three linen bands, and, placed in a coffin, was buried only a foot deep so as to be the more readily disinterred. The head had been put in a little wooden box at the top of a pole. The mayor Ly-Vûng had a box made exactly similar, hoping to substitute it for the other, and thus to get possession of the precious relics. But it was found impossible to cheat the vigilance of the guards. We had then to resort to another expedient. The gaoler, charged with

the care of the head, was promised a silver bar if he
would let us throw the head into the river in our own
way. This man, nothing loth, came at night on the
fourth day, to facilitate the matter. But God permitted our plans to be upset by a little mandarin of
Balliage, a young wolf of twenty-three, whose only
idea of government was to devour his people,—his
royal blood enabling him to do this with impunity.
This man sent one of his household to superintend
the projection of the head into the water. Our old
friend, Huong-Moï, had fastened a fish-hook in the
ear, with two hundred yards of line and a floater,
and persuaded the mayor to throw all together into
the river, thinking that the float would enable us to
discover it easily on the morrow. But the frightened
mayor threw the head in without detaching the line
from the boat, and after pulling a few strokes, the
head naturally following, at the alarm that the mandarin was coming he shook the line violently, the
hook got loose, and the head sank to the bottom of
the stream. All our endeavors to recover it the next
day were in vain. But God managed it for us in
another way. On the 15th of February some pagan
friends of Ly-Vûng, rowing down the stream, per-
ceived something floating on the water about four
leagues from the place of execution. They took it up
and found it to be our dear martyr's head. The good
mayor, Ly-Vûng, hastened to take it to his house, and
sent for Father Tinh, who instantly recognized it.
They wrapped it carefully in a white silk bag and
placed it in a vase which they sealed with tar. When
the good priest sent me word of what had occurred,
I desired him to bring the head to me, and the precious
relic arrived on the 24th of February. I opened the
vase in the presence of five witnesses: the head was

incorrupt. I took the little white bag in which Ly-Vûng had enveloped it, and in which it had been for nine days; from the right ear I took out the fish-hook which Huong-Moï had fastened in it and which had remained with about an inch of the line. It had made a wide opening in the ear as by a violent wrench. The condition of the flesh around the ear showed how it had been hacked by the inhuman executioner. I cut off some of the hair with my scissors, keeping five or six locks for his family. I tearfully turned this much-loved head in my hands, and finally replaced it in its urn, and deposited it in a neighboring house at the earnest entreaty of the inhabitants, finding it impossible at present to do with safety what I had wished, namely, to reunite the head to the other members. For this we must wait for a time of peace."

Bishop Jeantet, under the impression that the martyr's father was still alive, wrote to comfort him, declaring that Theophane, by his great merits, had well deserved the martyr's palm and adding that the Blessed Virgin, to whom he had ever been so tenderly devoted, had thus glorified him in the eyes of the whole world.

Bishop Theurel added in conclusion:

"My dear friends, shall I say that we are rejoiced or afflicted at your dear brother's glorious end? In one sense we all rejoice at his triumph, blessing and praising God for His choice; but for my own part, I cannot help feeling deeply the separation which has taken place. I am still quite young, being of the same age as our dear Theophane; our warm friendship and entire conformity of views on all points, made him a powerful auxiliary in all my labors, and a sharer in all the cares and anxieties of the future. Your brother was at least one-half of my strength and of my courage. He had the greatest prudence and wisdom,

united with a burning love and zeal. It seemed as if
he and I together could do great things in this Tong-
king vineyard; but alone, how shall I get on? His
departure has cast me down terribly and has upset all
my hopes and plans. I have cried for him bitterly,
and shall cry still more, whatever people may say! I
have said that he had an immense zeal for souls; also,
though his health was more delicate than that of any
other missioner in the diocese, he did more work than
anybody else, passing half the night, and sometimes
the whole day besides, in the confessional. His confidence in God was boundless and made him bold almost to a fault in his undertakings. While he was
working so admirably at Kê-Bêo in June, I wrote him
that he must take greater precautions, for the heavens
were big with clouds. He answered me with that
holy boldness which was one of his characteristics,
that not a hair of his head would fall unless by the
will of God. In truth, our Lord had determined the
hour of his martyrdom, and his happy fate was fore-
told him in 1851.

"He was a wonderful linguist and had completely
mastered the difficult Annamite dialect. He translated
the 'Concordantia Evangelica' of M. Migne into good
Annamite, as well as the Acts of the Apostles. He had
just completed the translation of the Epistles and of
the Apocalypse; and was in the midst of an abridged
Commentary from that of Picquigny, when he was
arrested. These two last translations, of which no one
had a copy, have, to my great despair, been burned,
not by the chief who took him prisoner, but by the
Christians of Kê-Bêo, whose fears had really troubled
their reason. Another of our Christian missions has
been more faithful to the memory of our dear brother.
I mean that of Bût-Dông, where he lived for eighteen

months with Fr. Saiget. This whole parish has been
for more than a year in open war with the mandarin,
Nam-Xang, whom your brother reproached so vehe-
mently from his cage. This functionary came himself
to Bût-Dông to force the people to trample the Cross
under foot; but the whole population having unani-
mously refused to apostatize, he was forced to yield
to the resistance of eighteen hundred men; and although since then he has issued edict after edict, he has
done nothing but lose both his time and his trouble.
. . . Bishop Jeantet had expressed the wish that when
the time came for the re-establishment of the seminary,
Theophane would become Professor of Theology.
'I hoped so much,' writes His Grace, 'from his
wonderful piety, zeal, and science. But the Sovereign
Arbiter of all things has decided otherwise—*"Fiat
voluntas tua."* ' The faithful widow Nghiên," continues Bishop Theurel, "brought back the clothes and
chain of our dear brother and handed everything
over to us. A little later we hope to send to Paris the
chain, the little bag, and the fishhook of which I have
spoken, together with the hair, one or two autograph
letters of the martyr, and the linen soaked with his
blood.

"The ring which went about the neck is wanting
to the chain, having been appropriated by the brother
of the mandarin, as was also one of the foot rings.
I will forward to you, my dear Eusebius, as well as to
M. Henry and Mdlle. Mélanie, your portion of his
hair, and of the linen soaked with his blood. I do
not send these things to-day, as my parcel is already
too heavy; I must wait for the next time. A little
later I hope also to send you each some little remembrance chosen from among his effects. Bishop Jeantet

and I—and I doubt not all our brethren—will consent that his precious martyr's chalice shall pass into your hands.*

"The catechist, Khang, who was seized with your brother, was exiled into the province of Hông-Hôa, which belongs to the Western Vicariate. But before starting, he was allowed to go and venerate the head of his spiritual father, which was still exposed. This was on the 4th of February. The chief of the canton, Dô, in addition to the recompense of thirty bars given by the king, received four bars from the mandarin prefect, and has been created a mandarin of the ninth class.

"After the martyrdom of your dear brother, I learned the news of your father's death. So I do not address this letter to him, but to you all. . . . .
†*Beati qui lavant stolas suas in sanguine Agni!*"

(*Note of the Family.*—On the 25th of March, 1865, Bishop Theurel wrote as follows on the subject of the relics, to M. l'Abbé Eusebius Vénard, curate of the Cathedral at Poitiers:—"The whole of your dear brother's body, except the head, arrived at Hong-Kong on the 1st of March, and started for France by the ship 'St. Vincent de Paul.' It will arrive at the end of August or in the beginning of September, by Nantes. With the body I have sent the chalice and other precious remembrances."

"Under the same cover, Bishop Theurel, foreseeing our impatience, sent us each a portion of the relics,

*The letters written from the cage by Theophane Vénard to his family were hanging on the wall of the guest room in the presbytery at Assai, when the writer visited Fr. Eusebius. In one corner of this room was a cabinet, a family heirloom, in which were kept the martyr's chalice and many other relics and souvenirs.

†Blessed are they who wash their stoles in the blood of the Lamb.

contained in three little packets, sealed with the
episcopal seal, and marked with the following in-
scriptions, written in the Bishop's own hand:—*Hair of
M. T. Vénard. Linen imbued with his blood. Small
bones, cartilages, nails, etc."*)*

*The head of Theophane Vénard is in Tong-king, an object of ardent
devotion to the native Christians. It was exposed for veneration while
the Beatification was taking place at Rome in 1909. Through the great
kindness of a bishop in Tong-king, a portion of the neck-bone is to-day
treasured in the American Foreign Mission Seminary at Maryknoll,
Ossining, New York.

The hair and linen referred to in the "note of the family" were at
Assai until the death of Fr. Eusebius in 1913. Little by little, however, he had disposed of a great part of these relics to clients of the
martyr, among others to the "Little Flower of Jesus," the young Carmelite of Lisieux whose devotion to Blessed Theophane was one of her
dying consolations.

To satisfy his "importunate friend from America, whose letters
were like telegraphic dispatches," the good old priest was twice pre-
vailed upon to part with some small portion of these precious treasures,
although it must be confessed he did so grudgingly enough.

The chain worn during the martyr's captivity is in a cabinet devoted
to Theophane Vénard in the Hall of Martyrs, at the Missions Étrangères, Paris. The body reposes in a crypt under the Seminary Chapel,
and is indicated by a tablet placed at the left side near the entrance.

The Mission House, known in Paris as the Missions Étrangères, is
reached from the Rue du Bac, No. 128. The arched doorway, which,
it may be well to remember, faces the Bon Marchè (a well-known department store), is quite inconspicuous, since it is crowded between
commercial establishments, the Seminary itself, as well as the chapel,
being located away from the busy thoroughfare and behind these
buildings.

The Hall of Martyrs is not always open, and there is no inclination
on the part of the Seminary Directors to encourage the merely curious
visitor. To those who are interested in the mission cause, however,
and who, as such, would probably appreciate the priceless souvenirs of
modern martyrs, a welcome is always given, and every possible courtesy
extended, especially if they are strangers from afar.

CHAPTER XV.

First Anniversary and Retrospect.

THE official news of Theophane Vénard's martyrdom did not arrive in France till the end of December,
1861, nearly eleven months after the event. The
Bishop of Poitiers at once resolved to hold a feast in
honor of one whom his hand had led into the sanctuary, and who had become the glory of his diocese
by the heroic confession of faith and the shedding of
blood for Jesus Christ.

The feast was fixed for Sunday, the 2nd of February, the Purification of the Blessed Virgin, and the
anniversary of the martyrdom. The bishop came to
preside at the ceremony in the church of St. Loup,
the native parish of our hero. He was accompanied
not only by the members of his own chapter, but by
about a hundred priests, friends or companions of
Theophane, including the Abbé Dallet—who had been
compelled from bad health to return to France for a
few months—and the superior of the Seminary of
Foreign Missions at Paris.

After the Mass, the bishop preached with such fervor and emotion that the whole audience was in tears.
Yet there was nothing sad about the festival. As a
priest who was present said, "In each martyr, grace

assumes a different character. In Theophane it was an indomitable serenity, a joyous calm which nothing could disturb. One may say of him as the English do of one of their poets, 'He was born with a rose-bud on his lips and a bird to sing in his ear;' so graceful was his imagery, so melodious his words. His natural sweetness spread a charm over everything and every one with whom he came in contact. Even at the last moment of his life he poured it out on those who pressed around his cage, on the instrument of his torture, on the very earth which was to drink his blood. We feel as if the fatal blow which severed that dear and venerated head were only as the pressure which separates from its stalk the fair flower that is to adorn the altar." This joyous calm in the martyr's character, so well known to his parents and townspeople, had colored the festival held in his honor. Nothing spoke of death; but everything breathed hope and life.

His father's house was decked with flowers that day as for a marriage feast; and at the breakfast given by his brothers, the room was hung with festoons and garlands, the martyr's monogram being twined with palm branches and crowns.

Mdlle. Mélanie Vénard assisted at the feast. She had now followed her heart's desire, so often talked over with her martyred brother, and had taken the veil in the Convent of the Holy Family, under the name of "Sister Theophane."

Towards the end of dinner, the Abbé Chauvin, curate of St. Jacques de Châtellerault, read a hymn in honor of the martyr, the graceful and tender poetry of which provoked murmurs of approbation from the bishop and all the assembled company. Between the services, a large number of Theophane's old friends

INTERIOR OF THE PARISH CHURCH
at St. Loup.

made a pilgrimage to the grassy hillsides of Bel-Air, where the first inspiration for the foreign missions had come into his childish heart.

The wax taper carried by the bishop on that occasion was left, at his request, as a memorial in the parish church, and by its side hangs in a square frame an autograph letter of the martyr, written with a paint brush in his cage.

And now that we have followed Theophane Vénard from his birth to his death, is our interest in him entirely at an end? If our minds have been for a short time turned from frivolous thoughts to the contemplation of a life so pure, so holy, so single-minded in the dedication of all its gifts and powers to God, will it not have some influence, some effect on our future conduct?

We feel confident that our Lord will not allow so eminent an example to pass unheeded, and that already this martyr's words have kindled in other souls a like burning love and zeal for the conversion of the heathen. Scarcely had Theophane Vénard reached Tong-king when his letters began to fire the ambition of friends and companions, determining them to share in his apostolic labors for the foreign missions. We trust that on those who read this little book a like impression may be made; that if all cannot actually take part in the missioner's life, they may at least help others to do so by propagating the works of the foreign missions to the utmost of their power in the circle of their own homes.

At the Congress of Malines a noted Catholic orator, M. Augustin Cochin, after having pronounced

14

an eloquent discourse on the progress of science and
arts from the religious point of view, quoted a letter
of Theophane Vénard to enforce his arguments, and
to induce the eminent men who listened to him to
join in a series of resolutions, of which the first was,
"To labor incessantly for the *propagation of the faith
among the heathen.*" He went on to say, "I cannot
understand that any true Catholic should refuse to
work energetically for the maintenance of those model
men amongst us who go forth to regions where the
Gospel is unknown and seal the truth with their
blood. Their words breathe a faith and an ardent
charity of which their lives and their deaths are the
proof. . . .

"I was struck the other day by an unexpected coin-
cidence between the letters of two men to their sisters, both delicate and sincere, both written in presence of the tomb, one by a brother to his sister who
is dead, the other to his sister by a brother about to
die. The former was from a man but too well known,
who, searching in his heart for what was purest and
best, could speak only of 'refined doubts,' 'delicate
questions,' 'tears mingled by the women of old with
the waves of Biblos,' 'the mysteries of Adonis,' . . . .
and thus he writes to her whom he calls his 'good
genius!' The other was written at midnight by a prisoner from his cage on the eve of martyrdom, on the
20th of January, only two years ago, at the very
moment, gentlemen, when some of us were probably
at a ball." . . . He then read aloud the letter to
Mélanie, and added, "Gentlemen, between these two
letters of Rénan and Theophane Vénard, between the
two doctrines which they inspire, between the two
states of mind which they reveal, my choice is made;

gentlemen, I earnestly recommend to you the work of the propagation of the faith!"

The whole Congress was moved by these eloquent words; and the letter, which M. Cochin termed "One of the most beautiful pages in the History of the Martyrs of the Nineteenth Century," produced in the hearts of his three thousand auditors an emotion which bore immediate fruit, for the next day the orator received, among other offerings, without any signature or sign of the donor, a bank note of one thousand francs for the Foreign Mission Seminary.

Let us hope that this generous heart may find its imitators; and that this humble biography, however feebly executed, may move other Christian souls to come forward and help in the great work.

Retrospect.

When the storm of persecution which marked the death of Theophane Vénard had spent itself, it was found that, between the years 1857-1862, in the various parts of Tong-king and Cochin-China, 117 foreign priests were martyred. In addition to these, 115 Annamite priests—one third of the native clergy of Annam—poured out their blood for Jesus Christ. Eighty convents were destroyed and 2,000 Annamite nuns dispersed, 100 of whom gave up their lives for the faith. All of the colleges were closed and most of the catechists and pupils arrested. The more prominent among the native Christians, to the number of about 10,000, were also put in prison. Of these, more than 5,000 died for the faith,—some being decapitated after regular trial; others burned in groups, buried alive or drowned. In Tong-king, the mandarins, foreseeing that liberty would soon be proclaimed, cut off completely the supply of food and caused many to die of starvation.

A period of peace followed in Tong-king, with occasional threatenings, until 1882, when Father Bechel was beheaded with his catechists and his flock. The royal council then considered a general massacre of all Catholic priests and people. The king, Tu Duc, the same under whom Theophane Vénard was sentenced, opposed the movement. Shortly afterwards he died, after a reign of thirty-five years,—a reign that had been often criminal and always unhappy.

Another frightful massacre took place in 1885, covering the whole region of Indo-China. In the mission of Tong-king 163 churches were burned, 4,799 Catholics were killed, and 1,181 died of hunger and misery.

To-day France is in peaceful possession of Tong-king and the great persecutions have ceased. The following statistics, supplied from the latest report of the Paris Seminary will be of interest to the reader, who cannot fail to see here again exemplified the well-known axiom of Tertullian, "Sanguis martyrum semen Christianorum"—"The blood of martyrs is the seed of Christians."

Tong-king in 1912.

Catholics	406,859
Churches or chapels	1,475
Bishops	6
Missioners (European)	146
Native priests	294
Catechists	1,045
Seminaries	9

Students	873
Community of men	1
Religious	16
Communities of women	49
Religious	640
Adult pagans baptized	3,125
Children of pagans baptized in danger of death	30,387
Children of Christians baptized	10,763
Schools	1,126
Pupils	33,600
Orphanages and Infant Asylums	31
Children in the same	4,334
Workshops	17
Children in the same	492
Dispensaries	45
Hospitals	21

The writer is now in occasional correspondence with a young missioner whom he met at the Paris Seminary and who has since been sent to Tong-king. Some months after his arrival this young priest wrote:

"It is a little more than a year since I announced to you my call to the priesthood and my approaching departure for the missions. The mission chosen for me is familiar to you through the life of Theophane Vénard, of whom we spoke so much during your stay at the Missions Étrangères, Paris."

"Well, I am in the mission where so many martyrs have labored,—the mission of Tong-king. My joy, or rather *our* joy (for there are two of us—Father De Coomay and myself), was all the greater on our arrival, because we had been a long time sighing for the day. In fact, the voyage was not a very happy one. In place of thirty days,—the usual passage,—it took us forty-five days to get to Tong-king. We had two accidents to the machinery during the trip, and just as we were entering the Tong-king River our boat struck on a hidden ledge.

"Happily the sea was calm and the day following the shipwreck a boat came to rescue us. There were no deaths to deplore, but a considerable portion of our baggage is at the bottom of the sea. I lost nearly all my books and many little souvenirs of home. Father De Coomay was no more fortunate than I. God evidently wished us to practise detachment from the things of this world as soon as we arrived here. We are thankful to have escaped, as the boat went to pieces soon after we left it.

"On the boat were eight missioners; two for Cochin-China, and six for the three missions of Tong-king. I am in the mission of Maritime Tong-king, with Father De Coomay for my companion.

"At Phat Diem, where the Bishop lives, I was much pleased to meet Theophane Vénard's catechist, that is to say, the native who taught the language to the martyr. He is very old and bears the signs of his religion. These are the marks which the pagans made on the countenances of Christians at the time of persecution. The only occupation of the good old man is to prepare himself for death. He is always wrapped in silence, meditation and prayer.

"In this mission of Maritime Tong-king, there are 80,000 Christians. In the parish where I am, there are more Christians than pagans, and they are fervent Christians, too.

"On last Corpus Christi we had a beautiful procession. The Christians had worked many days to prepare a fitting passage, and with triumphal arches, oriflammes, etc., nothing was wanting for the cere-

mony. Then came numerous fireworks, for no event
can be solemnized here without fireworks. I have
been deeply moved by the faith of these Christians,
some of whom are descendants of the martyrs. They
recite the prayers with loud voices. Just now I am
studying the language. I have already preached
several times but I cannot yet converse fluently with the
natives.

"I recommend myself and my mission to your
prayers. With kindest regards, I am

"Most sincerely yours,

"MATTHEW ROCHER,

"Missionary Apostolic,

"Phat Diem, Tong-king."

These lines have a familiar ring. They bring back
the earlier days of Theophane Vénard, who after all
was only one of many,—a type which is being perpet-
uated in the Catholic Church.

A few years ago, Basil Huctin, a parishioner of
Eusebius Vénard and one of three brothers all of
whom have devoted their lives to the foreign missions,
wrote to the editor a farewell letter on the eve of
his departure from France. The spirit which breathes
through these lines is the same as that which shines
with such lustre in the life of Theophane Vénard.

"I know that you are interested in my future
mission and I am now able to announce it.

"The better part has been chosen for me. Coming
from the diocese of Poitiers, from the land of Theophane Vénard and Blessed Cornay, and as a parishioner
of Fr. Eusebius Vénard, I am booked for *Maritime
Tong-king*.

"If I must regret not being able to assist in Paris
at the solemnity of Theophane's Beatification, I am

amply compensated by the opportunity which I shall have to make a pilgrimage to the scene of his martyrdom, to venerate his head, which, you know, was left at Tong-king, and then to celebrate Mass on the day of the solemnity.

"Have I not reason to believe that I have drawn the best lot of all? And may I not hope for the powerful intercession of our dear martyr, to whom I owe my sweet apostolic vocation and the special favor of being sent to Tong-king? Am I presumptuous in expecting his constant intercession, and if not the crown of martyrdom, at least the crown of Heaven, the reward promised to the conquerors.

"More than ever do I need fervent prayers, that I may be a missioner such as were those of past generations—who, worthy of martyrdom, have made the Society and religion illustrious by the shedding of their blood. Fifty years—sixty years, after these, we come, their imitators, to gather the harvest on the soil which they prepared, sowed and watered. May we have fruit as abundant!

"The mission to which I am assigned is a new foundation, established in 1900. Out of two million inhabitants there were 90,000 Catholics last year. The thirty missioners on the ground baptized 8,263 pagan infants and 1,371 adults,—a fine sheaf, is it not, to present to the Father of the family?

"The extraordinary number of pagan infant baptisms is due especially to an awful rice famine in which numerous families perished from hunger.

"In conclusion, I beg your prayers, to soften the grief of my family caused by separation. My beloved father and mother are old. The day when they would have realized their most precious dream—to see their

children priests—will see them depart with no hope
of a reunion until we meet in Heaven. Their hearts
are already bruised by the departure of my brother
Alfred, who left on the 11th of September, and in two
weeks more, the sacrifice will be repeated. May God
give me strength and courage.

With sincere regards, I am, as ever,

Yours in Our Saviour and Mary Immaculate,

BASIL HUCTIN, M. AP.,

of Maritime Tong-king."

"P. S.—I was with my family from Oct. 19th to
Nov. 1st. The good-bye is over, eight days ago. My
father and mother suffered keenly when I was going,
but they had accepted the sacrifice long before and
generously offered it to God for His glory, for their
own salvation and for the salvation of souls. May
the Blessed Virgin soften for them the grief of
separation. It is to her motherly protection that I
have confided them. I am simply waiting now for our
departure from Paris.

"Oh! how happy I am, and how proud to have
received this beautiful mission of Tong-king! I could
not reasonably be otherwise when I consider the links
which bind me to Theophane through his venerable
brother.

"To give you an idea of the joy which filled the
soul of Fr. Eusebius Vénard when he learned that I
was destined for Tong-king, I will say that he could
hardly express it in words or by his letters. The
best proof of his satisfaction is that he wishes to be
present at my departure. In spite of his advanced
age he does not fear to make the journey.

"I am going to ask, with insistency, prayers for
the young missioner of Maritime Tong-king, for his
work and above all for his sanctification.

"The choicer and more beautiful my inheritance, the greater is my obligation to care for it with zeal and love. Pray that I may be a holy missionary priest. God and our blessed Mother will do the rest for me.

"Be assured that on my part I will not forget you. I will unite my prayers with those of my Christians for all who are included in your intentions.

Affectionately in Our Lord and Mary Immaculate,

BASIL HUCTIN,

M. Ap."

To-day other young apostles are walking in the footsteps of Theophane Vénard. These will follow the path marked out for them, and, if necessary, they too will cheerfully bend their heads to receive the sabre-cut of the persecutor; and when the tidings of their martyrdom shall have reached the Mission House which nurtured them, a joyous hymn of praise will be sung, and that night in the dark silence of the sanctuary, scores of young aspirants will pray with renewed fervor, each asking as a special grace, that he, too, may be *fortunate* enough to win the martyr's crown.

The age of martyrs will never pass in the true Church of Jesus Christ.

FR. EUSEBIUS VÉNARD, AT FORTY YEARS OF AGE.

CHAPTER XVI.

The Afterword.

The reader will naturally wish to know what became of the several members of the Vénard family, to each of whom in turn the martyr's letters were addressed.

In the editor's preface mention has already been made of Eusebius, who was for many years the beloved Curé of Assai. Fr. Eusebius died on February 24, 1913. In the course of the narrative it has been learned that M. Vénard, the father, died before receiving news of his son's martyrdom, and that Mélanie —shortly afterwards—entered a religious order, "Les Religieuses d'Espérance.

Mélanie, Theophane's *second self,* as he often called her, died in the convent at Amiens, in France. Henry married, but after a few years lost his wife and only child. Until his death, a few years ago, he shared with Fr. Eusebius the humble presbytery at Assai. Their housekeeper, a gentle townswoman from the old home at St. Loup, remembered Theophane when, as a boy of fourteen, he pastured his father's goats on the hillside of Bel-Air. She recalled too his departure for the missions. In this simple household, aglow with the memory of a martyr and adorned with many souvenirs of his life, the writer spent happy and profitable hours. Towards the end of his life Fr. Eusebius did not enjoy the best of health, but only a few years before his death he produced a successful martyr-play in honor of his brother—the labor of many months.

This drama was enacted by the villagers of Assai in the spacious churchyard and drew a great assemblage from the surrounding country. A letter received at the time from Fr. Eusebius, acknowledging some photographs—the results, good, bad, and indifferent, of a forced attempt made by the writer during one of his visits to Assai—will throw light on this interesting Curé, while it gives information about the little drama in which he is so deeply interested. The reader will remark that the saving sense of humor is not lacking in the brother of Theophane Vénard.

"Assai (by Airvault), Deux Sèvres, France.
"Oct. 23, 1905.
"Reverend and dear Father:

"I have safely received your masterly efforts at photography, and I am waiting to see if I do not get a second package. For a first attempt these are not a poor showing. We might even call them a success, especially the one in which I am posing at the door of my presbytery.

"However, as a rule, the views of the surrounding country are more pleasing than the portraits, which are a trifle dark.

"All who have recognized themselves have been delighted, even Kébis,† although he is seen from

---
†M. Henry's dog.

behind; his master is truly proud of his pose. But there has also been much dissatisfaction in feminine circles (always inclined to jealousy), and my house-keeper is in the first rank, for she has failed to find her beautiful countenance.

"All the views of St. Loup are clear and distinct except the one of our homestead, which is a little dull. The pictures of Assai, taken from various points, are equally beautiful. The main altar, the dining room and your bed room are excellent.

"My health is about the same. I had some rather painful attacks in September and October, neverthe-less my work went on as usual. I have filled a large album of about four hundred pages with letters of the dear martyr, to preserve them as autographs. They are written from the College of Doué, the Seminary of Montmorillon, and the Grand Seminary of Poitiers. The following letters will fill two other albums.

"The drama, 'Captivity and Martyrdom,' is not yet in press. It is extremely difficult to find an editor. I hope later, by Christmas at least, to have it pub-lished.

"They speak of printing at Hong-Kong, at the Nazareth House of Foreign Missions, a selection of Theophane's letters. I will let you know about this later.

"Believe me always, dear friend,

Your very devoted and affectionate

L. E. Vénard."

Fr. Eusebius never tired speaking of Theophane, and with advancing years the thought of him became the strong undercurrent of his life. It was hardly possible to converse with the old gentleman for any length of time without drawing from his lips some reference to his beloved brother. He used to call him, rather proudly, *Le Venerable,* and later, more proudly, *Le Bienheureux* (the Blessed).

From time to time he visited Paris, staying at the Mission Seminary to arrange some of the many details incidental to the process of Beatification. He was always a welcome guest and an object of great respect to the students, all of whom loved Theophane.

Occasionally, too, he drove over to St. Loup to inspect the old home and to talk with the Curé about the days to come, when St. Loup would be a centre of pilgrimages and the relics of his beloved brother, guarded by friends, would be venerated by multitudes of the faithful.

Before returning to Assai, Fr. Eusebius would always walk out through the village, over the bridge that crossed the Thouet, to the hillside of Bel-Air. Here a simple monument still marks the spot where Theophane Vénard received his call to be a martyr.

A few yards from this monument, on a slight elevation, there has stood for many years, the stone apse of a memorial chapel. Good Fr. Eusebius pointed out to the writer this unfinished work, confessing, with a sigh, that the generosity of friends had failed him, and the chapel of which he had dreamed as a place of pilgrimage must wait for better times, or look to some other land for its realization.

That evening as we sat in his poor dining room at Assai, a gleam of hope came into the old priest's eyes, and he said, "Perhaps America will learn to love Theophane."

Closing Reflections.

That was in 1903.

Two years later the first edition of this life appeared and before Eusebius went to his reward he had the satisfaction of knowing that seven thousand copies had been printed and circulated, and that five and perhaps ten times that number of American people, young and old, Catholic and non-Catholic, had learned to love his blessed brother. He knew, too, that several young men and young women had been drawn to the religious life through the inspiration received from these letters and that the first vocations to the American Foreign Mission Seminary could be traced to the same influence.

America is beginning to know—and to know is to love—Theophane Vénard,—and not Theophane Vénard alone, but the noble army of heroes and heroines to whose company he belonged, and who, in our own generation, are struggling bravely for the Cause of Christ in fields afar.

English-speaking Catholics here in the United States and elsewhere have been accused, perhaps justly, of indifference to foreign missions. This accusation is met with the excuse that we have had too much to do at home; but the true Catholic, whose heart is all-embracing like that of Christ, knows that the solid development of the Church at home will be helped rather than hindered by our interest in its spread throughout the world, nay more, the one must depend upon the other. Love for the Church is like a flame, which if confined will die.

There is, indeed, much spiritual and material work to be done at home. There always will be; but if we wait until every home need has been met, we must wait till the end of time. Whatever may be said of the past, we are certainly now in a position to contribute at least a breath of prayer, a mite of alms, and some missioners—even though it be a proportionately small number—to the foreign missions.

We should remember that as yet, notwithstanding the clear command of Christ, uttered nineteen centuries ago, "Going, teach all nations,—preach the gospel to every creature," *there are at this moment more than 1,000 millions, out of the earth's population of 1,600 million, who do not know Jesus Christ.*

Remarkable progress has, it is true, been made in the last century towards the conversion of the world. This progress may be traced to the copious shedding of blood for Christ by men like Theophane Vénard and their converts, and to the establishment of systematic means of support for the missions, notably the Society for the Propagation of the Faith. As a result of these influences, spiritual and material, the Catholic Church to-day counts in the mission field, about 15,000 priests, 5,000 Brothers, and 45,000 Sisters, as against 1,000, all told, at the beginning of the last century.

This progress, however, can hardly be credited to English-speaking Catholics. On the contrary, we in the United States must confess with our confrères in England, "that as yet we have no heart for the heathen, and that zeal for the honor of God and the salvation of souls is less in proportion to numbers among us than among certain European Catholic peoples, upon whose shortcomings we are so ready to sit in judgment."*

These last words refer to our unhappy co-religionists in France, and the reader will more easily under-

---

*The Rev. Thos. Jackson at the Annual Conference of the Catholic Truth Society, held at Blackburn, England, in 1905.

FATHER EUSEBIUS VÉNARD IN 1905.

Assai, Deux-Sèvres, France.

stand the allusion when he recalls that *at the present
time more than one half of all Catholic missioners, and
one half of all monies subscribed to their support,
may be attributed to the generosity of the French
people.* If we must criticize the indifference of
French Catholics, let us admit that the divine note
of Catholicity in the true Church is due to-day largely
to self-denying sons and daughters of France, whose
sacrifices on the mission fields have won the plaudits
of an admiring world, and will yet, we believe, by
God's grace, enable France to triumph over present
trials.

Thank God, among the English-speaking people of
the world there are signs of an awakening to the mission needs. The apostolic zeal of the late Cardinal
Vaughan has blessed England with her Missionary
College at Freshfield and her Seminary for Foreign
Missions at Mill Hill, so that to-day this Society
which the Christlike heart of Cardinal Vaughan inspired, has missions in the Punjab and Madras, India;
in Borneo, New Zealand, and the Philippine Islands;
and in Uganda and the Congo of Africa. It counts
among its members three Bishops, two Prefects
Apostolic and nearly two hundred priests. It is true
that many of its missioners are not of English-speaking origin, yet they have been trained in England.
Mill Hill stands to-day as a witness to the aspirations
of a far-seeing hierarchy and an encouragement to
the missionary spirit of Catholic youth, while it holds
before all classes the high and inspiring ideal of the
apostolate, a most valuable asset in the life of the
Church.

In the United States we have until recently been
without such a national Seminary and the religious
orders that supplied foreign mission recruits from

15

other countries seemed to lose sight of this phase of Catholic effort in the presence of our many and varied home needs. Had we been asked, a few years ago, to direct some young aspirant whose heart was prompting him to *"go the whole way"*,—to give up home and country for Jesus Christ, we should have been at a loss to know where to guide his steps, unless away from our own land, to Mill Hill or to one or other of the seminaries on the continent of Europe. And in some of these he could not be accepted if he were not already familiar with the language of the country.

In 1905, when the first edition of *A Modern Martyr* appeared, we expressed a hope that the day was not far distant when this urgent want would be supplied, when the doors of an American Seminary for Foreign Missions should be thrown open to Catholic youth with world-wide hearts.

To-day, thanks to God, *the doors are open.* At Maryknoll,* high above the noble river along which Fr. Isaac Jogues, martyr for Christ, once sailed, a little group of pioneer American students are preparing for the foreign missions, blazing a trail that we have reason to believe many will follow in the years to come.

---

*The Foreign Mission Seminary at Maryknoll was opened to students in September, 1912. It occupies a splendid stretch of land—about ninety-three acres of farm and forest—thirty miles north of New York City, and lies partly in the town of Ossining and partly in New Castle. The elevation is 550 feet and from this height an eight mile sweep of the Hudson River is in view. The post-office address is Ossining.

In September, 1913, the new Seminary opened at Scranton, Pa., its first preparatory school. It is called the Vénard Apostolic School. Boys who have a special inclination for the foreign missions and who are ready for high school work are received here. The Seminary hopes later to establish preparatory schools in several other sections of the United States.

'And Maryknoll is not alone.

There are now in this country several branches of European orders or societies which have on their membership rolls "apostles in the field." The Congregation of the Holy Cross, whose headquarters are at Cornwells, Pa., has sent some of its priests to Africa, and from the house of the same Congregation in Notre Dame, Indiana, several have gone to India; the Brothers of Mary, at Dayton, and Franciscans from the St. Louis province are represented in Eastern missions; and we are inclined to think that other European missionary societies with branches here, e.g., the Missionaries of the Sacred Heart and the Marists, have one or more Americans (born or adopted) on their missions. If not, we are bold enough to say that they should spare a few for that purpose.

In this connection we note a thriving German organization, the Society of the Divine Word, which has its headquarters in Steyl, Holland.

This Society has founded a branch in the United States, at Techny, Illinois, and expects in time to send from our country a goodly number of zealous apostles to some one or other of its several missions.

The Church in America is at heart Catholic. Her children are generous and capable of great sacrifices for the faith which they treasure. As the knowledge of Catholic missions develops among us, the value of a missioner's sacrifice will be more fully appreciated, and we shall see in the Catholics of America constant proof of their devotion to such heroes as Theophane Vénard, and to the soldiers who to-day are struggling in martyrs' footsteps. The name of Theophane Vénard will yet find its proper place in our affectionate remembrance, alongside of names which have been hallowed for centuries; and if our preference must manifest itself, we shall hardly be blamed if we turn to one who faced and conquered the trials of our own day, and who died for Christ,—A *Modern* Martyr.

On May the 2nd, 1909, Theophane Vénard was declared Blessed. It was his brother's painstaking labor which prepared the facts leading to this declaration, and a letter from Fr. Eusebius to the writer, prepared in Rome on the day of the Beatification, expresses his joy on this solemn occasion.

"The great day had just come to an end and I wish to tell you my joy and my happiness and how much I have thought of and prayed for you.

"Yesterday and to-day, I have had emotions truly delicious and beyond all expression. Yesterday, the entire deputation from the diocese of Poitiers, in which St. Loup (the martyr's home) was notably represented, was received by Pope Pius X. in a very special audience.

"Before this audience, the Holy Father wished to receive me alone and to give evidence to me of his fatherly tenderness. He asked intimate details about dear Theophane and spoke to me with much satisfaction and praise about my own life-work, consecrated as it has been to the glory of my blessed brother.

"To-day was the great day of the Beatification, a ceremony grand and touching in the extreme. The chanting was very beautiful. I admired especially the Te Deum, during which I was many times suffocated by sobs and tears of happiness.

"This evening at five o'clock, there was another gathering at St. Peter's, where the Pope came to

venerate the relics of the newly Blessed and to assist
at the Solemn Benediction.

"The assemblage was immense, the great Basilica
filled to overflowing. All the Papal court was present
to participate in the ceremony and there was a splendid
illumination which brought out the aureoles of the
martyrs.

"When the Pope and his court had left the Church,
from the tribunes next to mine there rushed towards
me an avalanche of people, most of them unknown
to me, who offered congratulations, shook my hands
and kissed them with visible joy. In treating me thus,
they believed that they were in relationship with
Theophane himself,—as if he were living.

"I was happy in all these proofs of affection given
to the Blessed One in my person and the impression
they made was indelible, although my fatigue was
extreme.

Very affectionately yours in Christ,

L. E. VÉNARD,
Curé d' Assai."

A few months after the Beatification, impressive
ceremonies were held at Hanoi, in Tong-king, where
the martyr's head is preserved. Fr. Basil Huctin, a
parishioner of Fr. Eusebius Vénard whom we have
already mentioned in these pages, sent to the writer
a description of this celebration and added an account
of his pilgrimage to the scene of Theophane's death.

"At St. Loup the pious pilgrims could follow the
road leading to the hill of Bel-Air; but I have followed
the road which led to the martyrdom and triumph.
Sunday, after Vespers, in company with another
Father, I set out from the site of the old prison,
now demolished. Opposite is the Grand Mandarin's

former residence, with the judgment hall where the martyr was examined, bidden to trample the Cross, threatened with the *rotin,* and for a time imprisoned. We examined all these scenes, and a little prayer rose from our hearts to our lips.

"We proceeded on foot amidst an indifferent crowd, talking little, and only to stimulate memory. From the city gate we went in the direction of Red River, a little distance away. It is hard to discover the actual spot of the execution, for in the past forty-eight years the river has shifted, submerging different islands and claiming more land. We stood silently, among people who had no suspicion of the pilgrims' prayers, and mentally reviewed the scene—the great circle of two hundred soldiers formed around the young martyr, radiant with happiness; the removal of his garments, the same ignominy Our Lord suffered before being placed on the Cross. It seemed as if I could hear the sound of the hammers and pincers loosening the nails that fastened the rings at neck and ankles. Then, after the terrible preliminaries, came the picture of the hideous executioner performing his sad work, and the head rolling on the ground, deluging and fertilizing the Annamite soil with its pure blood.

"After all these thoughts had passed through my mind, I made a fervent prayer to the dead martyr, our protector and model in heaven—a universal prayer, for his venerable brother, for my family, friends, and benefactors, for the missions, for the conversion of the heathen and the spread of Christianity."

Blessed Theophane Vénard has already become to not a few, a special intercessor in Heaven. In the beautiful life of Sœur Thérèse (which appears in

English under the title "The Little Flower of Jesus"),
there is striking evidence of the young Carmelite's
devotion to our martyr. "I cannot look upon him,"
said this holy nun, "nor upon Our Lady, without
shedding tears." And again, "He is a little saint.
There is nothing out of the ordinary in his life. He
loved the Immaculate Virgin very much, *his family
too*. And so do I. I cannot understand those saints
who did not."

Sister Thérèse died in 1897 at the age of twenty-
four. She was one of five sisters, all of whom became
nuns, daughters of M. and Mme. Martin, proprietors
of the well-known lace establishment at Alençon in
France.

The example of Sister Thérèse's devotion to Theophane Vénard has spread to many Carmelite communities and to several religious orders of men, in
which latter some of the younger novices have taken
the name of Theophane.

May this modern martyr inspire us all with deeper
love for souls and obtain for some among us the
blessed grace of a vocation,—if not to martyrdom,
at least to the world-wide Apostolate!

2 FEVRIER 1861

HYMN OF SISTER THÉRÈSE

(The Little Flower of Jesus)

To Blessed Theophane Vénard, Martyr.

Translated by S. L. Emery.

O Theophane, angelic martyr blest!
  All the elect to sing thy praise aspire;
And thee to hail, behold! there stand confest
  The seraphim, with love divine on fire.
I, a poor exile still on this dull earth,
  Cannot with them my joyful song combine;
Yet will I take my harp, and sing thy worth,
  And claim thee as a kindred soul to mine.

Thy brief, bright sojourn here was like a psalm
  Of heavenly melody, all hearts upraising;
Thy love for Jesus brought forth flowers like balm,
  Through all thy life thy dearest Saviour praising.
Writing thy farewell thy last earthly night,
  That farewell was a song of spring and love,
"I, little butterfly, the first take flight,
  Of all our loved ones, to our home above."

Thou, happy martyr! in the hour of death
  Didst taste the deep delight of suffering;
Thou didst declare, e'en with thy dying breath,
  That it is sweet to suffer for the King.
When the stern headsman made thee offer fair
  Thy torture to abridge, how swift thy word:
"Oh, blest am I my Master's cup to share!
  Long let my suffering last with Christ my Lord!"

Virginal lily! life had but begun,
  When Jesus heard thy loving heart's desire.
I see in thee a flower whose race is run,
  Yet His hand plucked it but to lift it higher.
And now, no longer, exile dost thou know;
  Thy ecstasy the Blest rejoice to see;
That Rose of love, the Virgin white as snow,
  Rejoices in thy heavenly purity.

Soldier of Christ! thy armor lend to me!
  For sinners' souls I long to give my life;
For them to give my tears, my blood, like thee.
  Protect me then, and arm me for the strife!
For them I fain would fight till life is done,
  God's kingdom take by force their souls to save.
"Not peace to earth I bring," so spake God's Son,
  "But fire and sword I bring." Oh, saving glaive!

How dear is now to me that pagan horde,
  The object of thy burning love below!
If Jesus would to me that grace accord,
  Ah, thither with what ardor would I go!
Before Him space and distance fade away,
  This earth is but a plaything on the breeze;
My actions, my small sufferings to-day,
  Can make my Jesus loved beyond the seas.

Oh, were I but a flower of springtime too,
  That soon the Lord would gather to His breast!
Come down from heaven at my last hour anew,
  O Theophane, thou youthful martyr blest!
Come, with the virginal flames of thy pure love,
  Come, to burn from my soul all earthly clay,
That I may fly to heaven's courts above,
  And join thy cohort in unending day.

CHANT OF DEPARTURE.

As sung at the Paris Seminary for Foreign Missions.

Words by FR. DALLET.

Music by CH. GOUNOD.

Par tez, hé rauts de la bon - ne nou - vel - le, Voi - ci le

jour ap - pe - lé par vos vœux; Rien dé - sor - mais n'enchaine vo - tre

zè - le, Par tez, a - mis, que vous ê - tes heu-reux! Oh! qu'ils sont

beaux vos pieds, mis-si-on - nai - res! Nous les bai-sons a-vec un saint trans-

port, Oh! qu'ils sont beaux sur ces loin-tai - nes ter - res Où

REFRAIN.

rè - gnent l'erreur et la mort! Par-tez, a - mis, a-dieu pour cet - te

vi - e, Por-tez au loin le nom de no - tre Dieu; Nous nous retrouve-

rons un jour dans la pa-tri - e, A-dieu, frè-res, a-dieu!

Qu'un souffle heureux vienne enfler votre **voile**,
Amis, volez sur les ailes des vents,
Ne craignez pas, Marie est votre étoile,
Elle saura veiller sur ses enfants.
Respecte, ô mer! leur mission sublime,
Garde-les bien, sois pour eux sans écueil,
Et sous ces pieds qu'un si beau zèle anime,
  De tes flots abaisse l'orgueil.

  Partez, amis, &c.

Hâtez vos pas vers ces peuples immenses ;
Ils sont plongés dans une froide nuit,
Sans vérité, sans Dieu, sans espérances ;
Infortunés ! l'enfer les engloutit.
Soldats du Christ ! soumettez-lui la terre,
Que tous les lieux entendent votre voix,
Portez partout la divine lumière,
    Partout l'étendard de la croix.

    Partez, amis, &c.

Empressez-vous dans la sainte carrière,
Donnez à Dieu vos peines, vos sueurs,
Vous souffrirez, et votre vie entière
S'écoulera dans de rudes labeurs.
Peut-être aussi, tout le sang de vos veines
Sera versé ; vos pieds, ces pieds si beaux,
Peut-être un jour seront chargés de chaînes,
    Et vos corps livrés aux bourreaux.

    Partez, amis, &c.

Partez, partez, car nos frères succombent,
Le temps, la mort, ont décimé leurs rangs ;
Ne faut-il pas remplacer ceux qui tombent
Sous le couteau de féroces tyrans ?
Heureux amis ! partagez leur victoire,
Suivez toujours les traces de leurs pas ;
Dieu vous appelle, et du sein de la gloire
    Nos martyrs vous tendent les bras.

    Partez, amis, &c.

Soyez remplis du zèle apostolique ;
La pauvreté, les travaux, les combats,
La mort ; voilà l'avenir magnifique
Que notre Dieu réserve à ses soldats.
Mais parmi nous il n'est point de cœur lâche,
A son appel tous nous obéirons,
Nous braverons et la cangue et la hache,
    Oui, s'il faut mourir, nous mourrons.

    Partez, amis, &c.

Bientôt, bientôt, nous courrons sur vos traces,
Cherchant partout une âme à convertir ;
Nous franchirons ces immenses espaces,
Et nous irons tous prêcher et mourir.
Oh ! le beau jour, quand le Roi des Apôtres
Viendra combler le désir de nos cœurs,
Récompenser vos travaux et les nôtres,
    Et nous proclamer tous vainqueurs !

    Partez, amis, &c.

En nous quittant vous demeurez nos frères,
Pensez à nous, devant Dieu, chaque jour ;
Restons unis par de saintes prières,
Restons unis dans son divin amour.
O Dieu Jésus notre roi, notre maître,
Protégez-nous, veillez sur notre sort,
A vous nos cœurs, notre sang, tout notre être,
    A vous, à la vie, à la mort.

    Partez, amis, adieu pour cette vie,
    Portez au loin le nom de notre Dieu,
Nous nous retrouverons un jour dans la **patrie**,
        Adieu, frères, adieu.

HYMN OF DEPARTURE.

Translated by S. L. Emery.

Ye heralds, bear glad tidings and God speed ye;
  Behold the day that your longing hearts have sought:
With zeal undaunted no dangers may impede ye;
  Depart, dear friends, for your happiness is bought.
The beauteous feet of Jesus' new anointed,
  We kiss with transports of holiest delight;
Tidings of peace, then bring to fields appointed,
  Where reign sin and error, dark as night.

REFRAIN

Depart, dear friends, for this life 'tis forever;
  The Name of God to distant peoples tell:
And we shall meet on high to part again, ah never;
  Farewell, brothers, farewell!

Dear friends, on wings of the wind ye'll soon be riding;
  May happy breezes then bear ye afar:
Fear not, for Mary her children e'er is guiding;
  Look up to her, to your hope, to your star.
Respect their mission, thou broad, mighty ocean,
  And bear them safe to their long journey's end;
Zeal so sublime should still your proud commotion,
  Your waves to their service swiftly bend.

REFRAIN

Oh! haste to reach those countries long forsaken,
  The people plunged in the darkness of night;
Without the truth, without God, they're overtaken,
  They hopeless fall into Hell in their plight.
Christ's soldiers, conquer for Him every nation,
  And may all men to your voices give heed;
Take ye the Light to every clime and station,
  Your standard's the Cross. Onward lead!

REFRAIN

In this career of your choice onward pressing,
  Give God your labors, your pains and your moil;
For ye will meet many trials sore distressing,
  Your life will pass amid hardships and toil.
Perhaps the blood in your veins warmly flowing
  Will all be shed; and those thrice blessed feet
One day, perhaps, in heavy chains be going,
  The tortures of pagans to meet.

REFRAIN

Depart, depart, your dear brothers are calling,
  For time a breach in their ranks oft has made;
Then go ye out to the stricken and falling,
  Render harmless the tyrant's sharp blade.
O happy friends, in their victories sharing,
  If ye will strive but their footsteps to trace,
God ye has called, and crowns of glory wearing,
  Our martyrs extend their embrace.

REFRAIN

Go ye with zeal of apostles all burning,
  To labors, combats, and poverty bare,
E'en unto death; it is these ye are earning,
  Behold the future God's soldiers will share.
Among us none has a heart that will falter;
  Obedient all, to God's call we would fly,
Happy to brave the hatchet and the halter;
  And, if we must die, we will die.

REFRAIN

And soon, oh! soon, we shall follow your traces,
  To seek for souls the true Gospel to teach;
We too shall cross o'er those vast, unknown spaces,
  To live and die for the Faith we shall preach.
Oh! blessed day, when with hearts overflowing,

At last the King of Apostles we meet;
Rich recompense for labors then bestowing,
　　As conquerors all He will greet.

REFRAIN

Tho' parting, still we shall claim ye as brothers,
　　Then think of us before God every day;
Let each unite in God's love with the others,
　　And thus united we'll labor and pray.
O God, O Jesus, our Master all-seeing!
　　Protect us, guard us, and watch our last breath;
Thine are our hearts, our blood, and all our being,
　　In life we are Thine, and in death.

REFRAIN

16

From Fr. Hudson, Editor of the Ave Maria.

"The third borrower has just returned the book. Thank you much and many times over for an autograph copy. What a charming volume it is!"

From Father Elliott, C. S. P., of the Apostolic Mission House, Washington, D. C.

"It is a most delightful book and very touching indeed. It filled me with envy for the high privilege of Vénard to die for the faith of Christ. I wish that every priest and every aspirant to the priesthood could read that book."

From the Catholic Fortnightly Review.

"These letters one might term models of the epistolary style, except that this expression seems too formal to apply to such natural, simple, and spontaneous communications. They are so real that the living voice of the writer seems to linger about the pages as one reads."

From His Eminence Cardinal Farley.

"I am very grateful to you for making me acquainted with 'A Modern Martyr'. I think it is the most fascinating book I have read in a long time. I can hardly put it out of my hands, and have finished reading half of it already. I have instructed the President of our Cathedral College to place a copy in the hands of each of our *petits seminaristes,* and I feel convinced that no better book could be given them for their spiritual reading."

Earlier Editions

From the Very Rev. F. Henry, of Mill Hill
College, England.

———

"Thanks, many times over, for Theophane Vénard, not only for the copy of the book itself, but above all for writing, publishing, and spreading it. It is bound to do an immense amount of good for the Cause which we both have so much at heart. The crowning glory will be when the United States of America starts her own Foreign Mission College, which I trust we shall both live to see. Before leaving Mill Hill, I gave the book to the Rector with instructions to have it read in the refectory."

———

From Mary E. Mannix (Author).

———

"I cannot tell you with what pleasure and edification I have read the life of Theophane Vénard. It takes one back from the twentieth century, with its terrible '*Zeitgeist*', to the ages of Faith, and makes one feel consoled to know that such souls are still born into the world.

"What a beautiful, natural, simple family, altogether! And how hard it must have been for the sweet, pure, affectionate boy to leave them behind! Nothing, nothing, but supernatural grace can explain it. And that feature of the book alone is a sermon and a lesson in itself. It seems to me it is the humanity of the saints, as that of our Lord, which brings them nearer to us."

From the Catholic University Bulletin.

"One cannot have too wide an acquaintance with noble Christian characters. In this age of ease, and of endless scientific discussion, of church-building, and of money-collecting, we need at times for our souls' sake to look to the example of the saints and heroes of God who are on the sterner side of life.

"Few biographies are better suited to remind us sweetly and forcibly of higher things than the volume presented to the public under the title, 'A Modern Martyr.' Modern, indeed, for it is within the lifetime of many of us that Theophane Vénard, a young priest of only thirty-two years, went smiling and singing to a martyr's death. Priest and layman, old and young, will find in this book much to delight the mind and to lift up the heart."

From the late Mary E. Blake (Author).

"Ever since I read that very beautiful memoir of a beautiful life which you have given the English-speaking people, it has been on my mind to tell you of the deep impression it left upon me.

"It is so unusual to have in the record of a saint, in addition to its spiritual atmosphere and its helpfulness towards reaching courage and steadfastness, such a memory of simple and sweet joyousness as the little book gives. It does not confound our poorer natures by its heights and depths—resplendent as those are in it. Something human and loving and intimate moves us to understanding and sympathy, and makes its appeal almost personal. You feel as if he would be friend as well as teacher. Thank you very much for making his story better known."

From the Catholic Transcript, Hartford, Conn.

"Here we have the life of a martyr brought right up to date—the story of a young priest, Theophane Vénard, who was beheaded for the faith in China some years ago. The Reverend Editor was naturally drawn to the theme before him by reason of his training under the lamented Abbé Hogan, late Superior of St. John's Seminary, Brighton, Mass., who was ordained in Paris on the same day as Blessed Theophane Vénard.

"'A Modern Martyr' has all the charm and interest of a novel. In variety of incident, in wealth of detail, in careful analysis of character, it will not suffer by comparison with the latest production of fiction. It is brimful of human love and human interest. Chapters there are that, strung together, might be woven into a sweet tale based upon domestic affection. Others there are that depict the development of the missionary instinct and its gradual unfolding and its final consummation in far-off China when Abbé Vénard's blood crimsoned the soil of Tong-king. Nothing so edifying and inspiring has of late been recorded in our missionary annals as the calmness and fortitude with which Theophane Vénard bent his neck under the stroke of the executioner's axe in testimony of the faith delivered by the saints."

From Bishop Casartelli, of Salford, England.

"When I was a boy of ten, I was taken by a good Belgian priest to visit the Missions Étrangères and the Salle des Martyrs. I shall never forget the impression of the latter, especially the sight of a young candidate kneeling at a priedieu and praying earnestly, probably for the grace of martyrdom.

"But I really knew nothing about foreign missions till 1870, when, on the day I received tonsure and minor orders, my mother gave me Lady Herbert's *Theophane Vénard,* still one of the treasures of my library. It is one of the few books I have wept over in reading. To it I owe my taste for and interest in foreign missions, and although the taste never led to anything practical, for I never had the personal call, it led among other things, to my becoming Editor of Illustrated Catholic Missions from 1889 to 1903, when I was compelled to give up the cherished post for the undesired episcopate. The editorship was the happiest avocation of my life.

"Judge, then, of my delight at receiving your admirable revised and augmented edition of my favorite book. You have done the work remarkably well. Pray accept my sincerest thanks and warmest congratulations. May this golden *Life* have a great circulation and stir up the missionary fire in many hearts."

A French edition of the life and letters of Blessed Theophane Vénard, as well as those of Just de Bretenières (martyr in Korea) and Blessed Pierre Chanel (martyr in Futuna) may be secured at the Catholic Foreign Mission Bureau, Maryknoll, Ossining P. O., N. Y.

The present work has been translated into Italian, under the title *Un Martire Moderno,* by the Rev. Paolo Manna, of Milan.

THOUGHTS FROM MODERN MARTYRS

Made up of short sentences from

Just de Bretenières
Blessed Theophane Vénard and
Henry Dorie—all 19th century martyrs and alumni of
the Paris Seminary for Foreign Missions.

Includes also a brief sketch of the life of each.

JUST DE BRETENIÈRES

This is a small book, suitable for occasional reading. It contains 122 pages, printed in large, clear type, and is illustrated with photographs of the three martyrs.

Price, in cloth, 35 cents. Postage 5 cents.

Address THE CATHOLIC FOREIGN MISSION BUREAU
Maryknoll, Ossining P. O., N. Y.

The Martyr of Futuna

(Blessed Peter Chanel, S. M., First Martyr of Oceania)

Adapted from the French by Florence Gilmore

"This simple life of Blessed Peter Chanel will do much to arouse enthusiasm for foreign missions, and will, we trust, lead many an American youth to labor in the 'field afar.' "—*The Catholic World.*

"A valuable addition to the Catholic Foreign Mission Society's list of publications.—A copy of this book in the hands of those interested in the missions may mean an increased number of vocations.—Catholic libraries especially should not fail to procure the life-story of this nineteenth-century martyr."—*America.*

Bound in cloth, 208 pp. 16 illustrations, $1.00 prepaid

Catholic Foreign Mission Society
Maryknoll, Ossining P. O., N. Y.

The Field Afar

ON the following pages our readers will find reference to **The Field Afar**. This paper is the organ of the **Catholic Foreign Mission Seminary**, now established in its permanent home at Maryknoll, Ossining P. O., New York.

The Field Afar began its mission in 1907 and has attracted world-wide notice. Its subscribers commonly assert that they read it **from cover to cover.**

Practical editorials, touches of missionary life that appeal to all classes, recent important happenings, and stories illustrating the apostolic spirit as well as life on the field,—these are the features, carefully grouped, that make **The Field Afar** a welcome visitor wherever it goes.

ASSOCIATE SUBSCRIPTION

Including a share in the works and suffrages of the
Catholic Foreign Mission Society

ONE DOLLAR A YEAR

SPECIAL RATES FOR SCHOOLS, SODALITIES, SOCIETIES, ETC.

For one year to any single address:

10 copies (for twelve issues)	....	$ 8.00
25 copies (for twelve issues)	....	20.00
50 copies (for twelve issues)	....	40.00
100 copies (for twelve issues)	....	80.00

ADDRESS: **THE FIELD AFAR**

Catholic Foreign Mission Seminary of America

Maryknoll, Ossining P. O., N. Y.

TRIBUTES TO THE FIELD AFAR

The Field Afar is excellent.—BISHOP CASARTELLI, *Salford, England.*

I am of those who read it from Alpha to Omega.—FATHER FORBES, *Superior of White Fathers, Quebec, Canada.*

It is certainly a well-edited paper. Do not fail to exchange with us.—REV. P. PAULO MANNA, M. AP., *Editor 'Le Missioni Cattoliche,' Milan, Italy.*

A completely new spirit,—an object lesson for the whole English-speaking world. God knows it was badly wanting.— REV. H. BROWN, S. J., *University College, Dublin, Ireland.*

I rejoice to learn that the work of the missioners is being made known in the United States through *The Field Afar.*— EDITOR OF ANTHROPOS, *Vienna, Austria.*

It is most interestingly conducted, the material and form equally admirable. There is a variety and life in it which our old countries in Europe have not yet known how to catch.— BISHOP MUTEL, *Korea.*

It is destined to promote a great and noble purpose, the work of building up Christ in souls. The work to be performed here is immense and only awaits missionary laborers and assistance, spiritual and temporal, from those to whom the Faith has been preached for centuries. *The Field Afar* deserves every encouragement and I shall recommend it to all our Catholics. —M. KENNELLY, S. J., *Shanghai, China.*

From the *"Catholic Transcript,"* Hartford, Conn.

The Field Afar is a powerful youngster already rejoicing in a large circulation of 15,000. It aims high and it is developing a rapid stride. We predict that, within five years, another cipher must be added to the three that stand at the right of the "15," in order to give an adequate idea of the wonderful growth of this most interesting monthly.

The success of the paper is an index to the progress of the movement which it represents. The Catholic Foreign Mission Society of America is in its infancy, but the cause to which it is consecrated is as old as the Church. The harvest is ripe and our people are not without the gift of apostolic charity. The prosperous Church of the United States will not be true to herself if she hesitates to take part in the perennial and Heaven-imposed task of evangelizing the heathen. The Mission Society has a glorious field and the laborers who have already entered it are cultivating the soil with zeal and with a prudence which gives earnest of a splendid harvest.

TRIBUTES TO THE FIELD AFAR

From "America."

The Field Afar, a monthly published in the interests of the Apostolic Seminary at Maryknoll, Ossining, N. Y., grows in attractiveness with each new issue. There are sixteen pages in this little publication, fourteen of them devoted to reading matter and two to notices and advertisements. A personal touch to all the articles puts *The Field Afar* in a class by itself. It is most readable and most instructive. . . . . In reading the issue for April, we thought what an excellent paper it is to put into the hands of our Catholic children, whether attending the parish schools or the Sunday schools.

The fulness of Christian charity is never to be found in the hearts of Catholics unless there be an expression of the desire to spread the Kingdom of Christ throughout the world, especially in those lands whose inhabitants are still sitting in the darkness of infidelity and the shadow of spiritual death. Our fathers did their noble share in spreading the Faith when they carried it as a sacred treasure from the land of their birth and planted it in all its vigor in the land of their adoption. That the apostolic mission of a former generation was well done, the marvelous expansion and present development in many States of the Union amply testify. The children of such sires, to be worthy of their lineage, must do their share in propagating the Faith, and for this purpose a knowledge of what is done or is planned to be done in mission fields is a prime necessity.

Day after day we read of the departure of Protestants, men and women, to foreign lands to join the truly astounding number of active workers belonging to the sects in all parts of the globe. The coffers of their missionary societies are being replenished by organized efforts to secure contributions, be they ever so small, from all the churches that dot the land, and by the colossal fortunes that are bequeathed for the furtherance of the same inspiring cause.

American Catholics give signs of waking up to that which is in itself a duty and the neglect of which will become a greater reproach if they are less zealous than such as possess only a tithe of that blessed heritage of the Faith which all Catholics possess in the fulness received from Christ and the Apostles. There are a score of ways in which zeal and interest in the great cause of missionary development may be manifested. One of the simplest and the most direct, in which even those may share whose income allows them to spend but little, is the support of a paper like *The Field Afar.* If the Catholic paper in the home is a perpetual mission, a paper treating of the missions is an inspiration, an inspiration to share the highest good that man can share with his fellow man.

From the *"Catholic Guardian,"* Jaffna, Ceylon.

The Field Afar is the very bright, sparkling organ of the Catholic Foreign Mission Society of America. We note with extreme pleasure the founding and progress of this Society and of its college for the training of American priests for the foreign missions. The young Church in America proves its vitality by the truly Catholic zeal with which it has taken up this noble work. We wish *Maryknoll* Godspeed, and may the example of the younger Church stir up the energies of her elder sister in the British Isles!

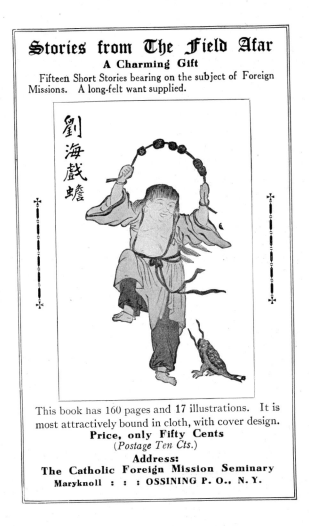

Field Afar Tales

A companion volume to the *Stories* already announced.

Twenty Short Stories, of which the Brooklyn *Tablet* says:

Up at the New Catholic Foreign Mission Seminary the purpose of educating the Catholic public of America in the matter of its duty to the foreign missions, goes on apace. Month after month the brilliant FIELD AFAR magazine comes from the printing-press to the homes of American Catholics and quietly fans the flames of enthusiasm. Already there is a glowing response in the material growth of this venture, while vocations among American youth and a broadened outlook on the world are even now in evidence. The monthly story of the missions, fresh from the Orient, is hardly surpassed by the bright little fictional tales that are written with an eye for propaganda.

The volume before us is the second collection of these breezy tales. It is most welcome and having a definite purpose, will, we believe, produce fruit.

The tales attributed to Fr. John Wakefield are clear and terse echoes of "what might have been" if American Catholics were interested in the evangelization of the Orient. Some of the stories are by a Teresian of Maryknoll. These also strike home and sound as if they were founded on fact. The many dramatic incidents that daily come to our shores from China and Japan, furnish the main theme of the tales, and the material is well handled.

NOTES

Binding . . . Cloth stamped in red
Pages 163
Full Page Illustrations . . . 16
Price . . . . . Fifty Cents
Postage . . . . . Ten Cents

Address:

The Catholic Foreign Mission Seminary
MARYKNOLL : : : OSSINING P. O., N. Y.

FOR FURTHER INFORMATION ABOUT CATHOLIC MISSIONS

General

Christian Missions ....*Marshall*
The Workers are Few ....*Fr. Manna*
Our Lord's Last Will and Testament ......*Dr. Ahaus*

Mission Work in America

(*a*) Biographical and Historical:
An American Missionary
Notes of a Missionary Priest in the Rocky Mountains
The Iroquois and the Jesuits
Catholic Pioneers in America—Murray
Over the Rocky Mountains to Alaska
Indian Sketches—De Smet
Sebastian Rasle
Life of Fr. Isaac Jogues, S. J.
Pioneer Priests of North America—Fr. Campbell
Across Wildest America—Fr. Devine
Western Missions and Missionaries—De Smet
Life of Bishop Machebeuf, Pioneer Priest of New Mexico, Colorado and Utah
Life of Very Rev. E. De Andreis, First Superior of the Congregation of the Mission in the United States
Missions of the Rocky Mountains
Missions among the American Indians
Fr. Lacombe—The Black-Robe Voyageur
(*b*) Stories:
The Story of a Mission Indian
Lot Leslie's Folks—Their Queer Adventures among the French and Indians

Foreign

(*a*) Biographical and Historical:
A Modern Martyr
Just de Bretenières
The Dominican Martyrs of Tonkin
First Martyrs of Holy Childhood—Lady Herbert
Travels in Tartary and Thibet—Huc
The Catholic Church in China—Rev. B. Wolferstan, S. J.
Life of Ven. Colin, Founder and First Superior-General of the Society of Mary
Life of Bishop de Mazenod, Founder of the Oblates of Mary Immaculate
The Lepers of Molokai—Stoddard
The Catholic Missions of Southern Burma
Thoughts from Modern Martyrs
Dominican Missions and Martyrs in Japan
The Cross in Japan
Japanese Martyrs
Missions in Japan and Paraguay
St. Francis Xavier
Missionary Labors of Mgr. de Mazenod and the Oblates
The Apostle of Abyssinia
(*b*) Stories:
Love Your Enemies (A Tale of the Maori Insurrection)
Prince Arumugan (A Tale of India)
Maron (A Youth of Lebanon)
The Queen's Nephew (A Story of Early Japan)
The Cabin Boys (A Story for the Young)
Children of Mary (A Tale of the Caucasus)
Laurentia (A Tale of Japan)
Chinese Lanterns—Alice Dease

The above lists have been prepared to suggest sources of information and interest. The supply of Catholic mission literature in English is scant, but a growing demand will doubtless stimulate the production of more books treating of this vital subject.

For further information address the:

CATHOLIC FOREIGN MISSION SOCIETY,
Maryknoll, Ossining P. O., N. Y.

REV. WILLIAM H. JUDGE, S. J.

AN AMERICAN MISSIONARY

(Third Edition)

THE STORY OF REV. WILLIAM H. JUDGE, S. J.

IN ALASKA

TOLD BY HIS BROTHER, A PRIEST OF ST. SULPICE

Introduction by His Eminence Cardinal Gibbons

•-•--•

THIS new edition of Father Judge's life and letters will be welcomed by all his friends and by the increasing number of those whose Catholic hearts beat in full sympathy with the intrepid missioners 'beyond the frontiers.' The headings of the chapters are enough to incite readers, who will wish to know more about the Yukon, Forty Mile Post and Circle City, the Rush to the Klondike and Dawson City. The excellent reviews of the first edition have been printed at the end of the present volume and bear testimony to the inspiring letters within.

•-•--•

304 pages. In Cloth. 20 illustrations.

Price, 50 cents. Postage, 12 cents.

CATHOLIC FOREIGN MISSION BUREAU

MARYKNOLL, OSSINING P. O., N. Y.

A LIST OF PAMPHLETS

The Mission Field of the Nineteenth Century—
Cardinal Moran
The Catholic Foreign Mission Field
English Catholics and the Foreign Missions
A Sister of Charity in China
Chinese Wayside Tales
More Chinese Tales
Cardinal Vaughan
St. Francis Xavier
Fr. Damien
Catholic Church in Japan
Martyrs of Japan
A Martyr of Japan (Fr. Mastrilli)
The Religions of Japan
St. Peter Claver (The Apostle of the Negroes)
Lazarus, an Indian Martyr
The Religion of China
An American Hindu on Hinduism
Catholic Missions
Catholic Missions in Japan
China and Korea
Jesuit Missionaries in Northern India
Don Bosco
Indian Languages and Early Catholic Missions
An Apology for Foreign Missions

For further information address the

CATHOLIC FOREIGN MISSION SOCIETY
Maryknoll, Ossining P. O., N. Y.

Recent Mission Literature

With Christ in China............Postpaid $1.00
By Rev. J. P. McQuaide, Ph. D.

Mission Literature in Foreign Languages

Théophane Vénard—in French............Postpaid $0.60

Un Martire Moderno....................Postpaid   .60
(Théophane Vénard in Italian)

Books under the patronage of Maryknoll

Vocations to the Priesthood......................$0.10
Rev. F. X. Steinbrecher

Abide With Me.................................   .25

Short Catechism of Church History...............   .25
Rt. Rev. Msgr. J. Oechtering

Why is Thy Apparel Red?........................   .60
Rev. M. F. Walz, C. P. P. S.

Bernadette of Lourdes.......................... 1.00
Translated by J. H. Gregory

The Church in Many Lands....................... 1.00
Rev. J. J. Burke

The Shepherd of My Soul........................ 1.00
Rev. C. J. Callan, O. P.

The Inner Life of the Soul...................... 1.50
S. L. Emery

New Psalter of the Roman Breviary.............. 1.50
Rev. L. C. Fillion, S. S.

Illustrations for Sermons and Instructions......... 2.00
Rev. C. J. Callan, O. P.

(POSTAGE EXTRA)

Address

The Catholic Foreign Mission Seminary
Maryknoll, Ossining P. O., N. Y.

Maryknoll Outfit
for Mission Training

Sold only to Sisters and others interested in Mission Training

Price $3.50.   Regular Price $7.00

Thoughts From Modern Martyrs .... $ .40
A Modern Martyr (Bl. Theophane Vénard)........ .60
Stories From The Field Afar .... .60
Field Afar Tales .... .60
An American Missionary (Fr. Judge, S. J., in Alaska) .60
Theophane Vénard (French) .... .60
The Martyr of Futuna (Bl. Peter Chanel, S. M.).... 1.00
Bernadette of Lourdes 1.00
100 Prayer Prints .... .25
Chi Rho Pin .... .25
100 Post Cards .... .50
Set of Educational Cards .... .50
Half-tone engraving of Bernadette of Lourdes ..... .10

Not including in above list but sold always at discount of forty per cent to Clergy and Religious:
With Christ in China $1.00

Catholic Foreign Mission Society
Maryknoll, Ossining, N. Y.

Bernadette of Lourdes

(Authentic portrait—Copyright by
PIERRE-BERNARD SOUBIROUS,
brother of Bernadette)

"A book of special interest to every American and above all to every American nun."—*Cardinal Gibbons.*

MISSION EDITION
Blue cloth, paper and binding of good grade, 14 half-tone illustrations $1.00

STANDARD EDITION
Paper and cloth binding, both of high grade, pure gold stamping, hand-printed photogravure illustrations. Boxed $2.50

DE LUXE EDITION
Dark blue suede leather binding, pure gold stamping and edge, hand-printed photogravure illustrations on real Japan vellum. Boxed $5.00

By special arrangement sold for the benefit of its work by

THE CATHOLIC
FOREIGN MISSION SOCIETY
MARYKNOLL, OSSINING, N. Y.